**RUDENESS
REHAB**

RUDENESS REHAB

Reclaiming Civility
In The Workplace
And Your Home Space

JOHN M. O'BRIEN, PH.D.

INDIE BOOKS
INTERNATIONAL

RUDENESS REHAB
Reclaiming Civility In The Workplace And Your Home Space

© 2025 John O'Brien
All rights reserved.
Printed in the United States of America.

No part of this publication may be reproduced or distributed in any form or by any means, without the prior permission of the publisher. Requests for permission should be directed to permissions@indiebooksintl.com, or mailed to Permissions, Indie Books International, 2511 Woodlands Way, Oceanside, CA 92054.

The views and opinions in this book are those of the author at the time of writing this book, and do not reflect the opinions of Indie Books International or its editors.

Neither the publisher nor the author is engaged in rendering legal or other professional services through this book. If expert assistance is required, the services of appropriate professionals should be sought. The publisher and the author shall have neither liability nor responsibility to any person or entity with respect to any loss or damage caused directly or indirectly by the information in this publication.

Stress in America® is a registered trademark of the American Psychological Association, Inc.
World Series® is a registered trademark of the Office of the Commissioner of Baseball
Kool-Aid® is a registered trademark of Kraft Food Groups Brands, LLC
Wordle® is a registered trademark of The New York Times Company
Skee-Ball® is a registered trademark of Bay Tek Entertainment, Inc.

ISBN 13: 978-1-957651-91-0
Library of Congress Control Number: 2024918881

Illustrations by JR Casas

Designed by Melissa Farr, Back Porch Creative, LLC

INDIE BOOKS INTERNATIONAL®, INC.
2511 WOODLANDS WAY
OCEANSIDE, CA 92054
www.indiebooksintl.com

Dedication

This book is dedicated to my mother, Carol Ann (Geggis) O'Brien, who was my first teacher regarding the importance of civility. "If you can't say anything nice, don't say anything at all."

Table Of Contents

Foreword ix
Prologue 1

Part 1: Rude! 7
Chapter 1 Rude! Why Should I Care About Incivility? 9
Chapter 2 The Incivility Within Us:
We Have Seen The Enemy And It Is Us 23
Chapter 3 Anger And Our Response:
Sure, "Everyone Else" Has A Problem 39

Part 2: Reclaiming Civility Within Ourselves 53
Chapter 4 Breathing: Even More Essential Than
We Realize 55
Chapter 5 Acceptance: How To Live With Our Emotions 69
Chapter 6 Four-Step Mindfulness: How To Handle
Our Reactions 83
Chapter 7 Compassion:
Searching For Another's Humanity 97
Chapter 8 Grounding: How To "Care Less" 113

Part 3: Reclaiming Civility With Others 125
Chapter 9 WAIT: Why Am I Talking? 127
Chapter 10 Active Listening:
Um, Did You Say Something? 143

Epilogue 163

Appendices	165
Call To Action	*167*
Acknowledgments	*175*
About The Author	*177*
Works Cited And Author's Notes	*179*

Foreword

One of my favorite colleagues at work, Dr. John O'Brien, has written an engaging book about incivility and how it permeates all aspects of our lives. This book sheds light on an important issue. Researchers are now saying incivility is becoming more prevalent than ever. Social disconnection has desensitized many to the impact of rude behavior. Dr. O'Brien, an educator and clinical psychologist, suggests this is a fixable problem. John likes to say: "Rehab is about a hope for things to get better and about taking the steps every day toward that better life."

I had the privilege of being one of the first readers of his manuscript and was "hooked" from Chapter One. Incivility is a growing problem in our society, and it's something that we all need to be aware of. John's book on this topic is incredibly insightful and informative. It helped me understand the impact that incivility can have on individuals and society as a whole. While reading it, I became much more aware of my actions and reactions to situations at work and at home, and I have tried to become more patient and mindful of my behaviors.

Today's social and political climate leaves many feeling hopeless about the future of our society if we continue to treat each other in these disrespectful ways. Yet, making the change is a daunting task. One of the things that I appreciated about this book is John's approach to the topic. He doesn't just focus on the negative aspects of incivility but also provides practical advice on how to deal with it. The book is well-researched with many concrete examples from John's personal life and professional practice. It provided a lot of useful information that I could apply to my own life.

John's writing style is engaging and easy to follow. He uses real-life examples to illustrate his points, which makes the book more relatable. I found myself nodding along as I read, and I felt like John really understood the challenges that people face when dealing with incivility. Many times while reading, I laughed out loud. I would love to attend one of John's sessions with a group of colleagues.

The rehab process may not be "pretty," and, at times, John says you may backslide into old behavior. However, I encourage you to trust John's process outlined in these pages. If you do, things can be better, and life can be less stressful for you and those around you. Anyone aspiring to reclaim civility will learn it is about choosing to respond differently to stressful situations, including the uncivil behavior of others. As you will explore in this book, reclaiming civility is not about becoming a doormat. Rather, it is about how to be skillful in navigating life and thereby minimizing your own stress.

As a leader at the organization I serve, I believe we all have a profound duty to help reshape the culture into one of mutual respect and civility. After reading this book, I feel more equipped to deal with incivility in my own life. I have a better understanding of what causes it and how to respond when I encounter it. I also feel more confident in my ability to help others who may be struggling with this issue. I have even used the final sentence in his prologue in teaching my

Organizational Behavior college course: "Every moment in life is a new chance for a reset and an opportunity to start fresh."

Dr. Brenda McAleer, Ph.D., CM, PMP
Associate Provost
Dean of the College of Professional Studies
Full Professor of Business Administration
University of Maine at Augusta

Prologue

"Hi, my name is John, and I can be uncivil."

"*Hi, John.*"

I would love to tell you that it has been five years and six days since my last episode of incivility, but that would not be true. Although I don't know exactly how long it has been, I am sure I have recently (and unwittingly) done something to hurt or offend someone.

Before you start pointing a finger at me, shaking your head, and saying, "Shame on you, John," guess what? *You have too.*

You see, we humans can be rude. All of us have the habit of behaving less than perfectly to others. When we're angry and stressed out, we exhibit behaviors that often do not reflect who we usually are. We get reactive, lose our patience, and then snap at someone (or worse). We can treat our fellow humans in a way that we would not want to be treated.

There is a direct connection between the level of our *stress and anger* and our rude behavior. I invite you to reread that last sentence and reflect on your own experience. Does that describe you?

Think about it. We get angry or stressed out, and it is like a switch is flipped—suddenly, we're being unkind. We all do it. Researchers say incivility is becoming more prevalent than ever. The social disconnection in our modern society, further amplified by the pandemic and social media, has created a world in which we are desensitized to the impact of disrespect and rude behavior on our own part and that of others. At the same time, these behaviors are having a negative impact on our stress levels, our relationships, and perhaps most importantly, our health.

A recent *Stress in America* survey by the American Psychological Association identified how most Americans continue to feel the long-term effects of the COVID-19 pandemic-related stress.[1] Studies also show that people around the world are exhibiting similar patterns of stress that then lead to rude and uncivil behaviors. One author in Australia created a new pseudodiagnosis to describe this phenomenon: "Post-Covid Rudeness Syndrome" (PCRS).[2]

It's as if anger, rudeness, and incivility are following in COVID-19's wake, like a new pandemic plaguing human interactions worldwide.

Even anecdotally, it seems like more of us are angry and stressed more often than before. In social interactions, wherever there is anger and stress, incivility (and just plain rudeness) follows. It adds up to the point where today's social and political climate leaves many of my clients, colleagues, and friends feeling hopeless about the future of our society if we continue to treat each other in these ways.

I've found the connection between stress and incivility true in my life, even before the pandemic. When I was younger, I was less skilled at managing conflicts and, at times, could become very uncivil, especially when I was stressed out. Whether out of anger or frustration, I said and did things that I wish I had not said or done. At times, I was one of *those* people.

In case you are thinking, "Wow, dude. How out of control were you? Did you make the national news? Were you in the police blotter? Do you have a rap sheet?" Fortunately, the answer to all these questions is *no*. I have never been out of control. People with anger problems can explode two ways—*out* or *in*. I exploded in and was much more likely to use cutting sarcasm, resentful silence, or (my favorite) passive-aggressive behavior. In other words, I was rude.

One of my mentors used to say, "The client can only go as far as the therapist has been." I took this idea to heart, and I have continued to work on myself with the goal of being of better service to my clients. Over the years, I've learned tools (which I describe in this book) to help clients reduce symptoms, manage stressors, and improve relationships. I have implemented these same skills myself for stress management and to recover from my bad case of rudeness. I offer them to you now as proven and effective ways to deal with "those rude people," including yourself.

Nowadays, when one of my clients tells me that they want to be like me because "you are always grounded," I quickly dispel the myth.

"I am not always grounded, and I do not perfectly practice what I preach." Psychologists are human beings, too. We often fall short.

However, I *do* constantly make efforts to practice what I preach. I *do* make efforts to be civil—or at least *not* be uncivil. Most days, I get a passing grade for being civil, with extra points for effort. It's taken years of effort to work on myself and develop self-awareness to change my "autopilot" tendencies toward incivility (and I remain a work in progress). I describe these combined efforts as "rudeness rehab."

> It's taken years of effort to work on myself and develop self-awareness to change my "autopilot" tendencies toward incivility (and I remain a work in progress).

What do you think of when you hear the term "rehab?" Stigmas associated with addiction have diminished over the years, but many people still have negative associations with anything related to substance use or recovery. I still have students who take my courses on addiction treatment say, "Addicts are just weak and using their addiction as an excuse for bad behavior." But weakness is never the real story—there is usually a mental health-related origin to someone's addiction. The same is true for incivility. The most successful rehab and recovery programs typically account for one's mental health as much as anything else.

Yet, whether it is addressing an addiction, adopting a new exercise program, or implementing organizational strategies in our lives, we as humans encounter difficulty when it comes to changing, even when it is in our best interest. We often need to be motivated to do so by the pain of what is known in the addiction world as "hitting bottom." People experience a "turning point" when the pain of change becomes less than the pain of keeping the behavior the same.[3] Is this true for you when it comes to dealing with incivility? Is our society "hitting bottom" with the "PCRS" pandemic, and are we all motivated to change? Time will tell, but you can at least begin with your corner of the world.

I tell clients all the time that making efforts to change and seeking help takes strength, not weakness. The journey to recovery is not easy, but it is worth it. Recovery from addiction often includes relapse to old behavior—I tell clients not to expect perfection from themselves but to learn from their mistakes.

Rehab is about hoping for things to get better and taking steps every day toward that better life. I also warn clients at the start of treatment about the risks associated with working on themselves, and I will now warn you, the reader, in the same way:

"Things often get worse before they get better."

When you finally stop and take an honest look at yourself, you may get overwhelmed, and life may get more complicated. However, you must trust the process and remind yourself of the end goal. It's the same process as "rehabbing" a kitchen or bathroom. Homeowners decide that they want to update a room, and they spend a great deal of time planning what they will do. Once construction begins, workers tear apart this room and create a huge mess, leaving the homeowner living in construction dust in the process. Having gone through several home renovation projects, I can attest to the fact that "living in chaos" is difficult to tolerate. Yet, bit by bit, the new room takes shape, and eventually, you can enjoy the beauty of the changes.

Why am I telling you all this? You are about to embark on a similar journey of "rehab" as you read this book. In *Rudeness Rehab*:

- You will learn about ways that you may engage in rude behavior yourself and be challenged (supportively) to consider ways to change and
- You will also be guided in how to deal differently with those uncivil and angry people who surround you at work, on the highway, or maybe even in your living environment.

The rehab process may not be "pretty," and, at times, you may backslide into old behavior. However, I would ask that you trust the process and maintain hope that things can be better and life can be less stressful for you and those around you.

Reclaiming civility is about choosing to respond differently to stressful situations, including the uncivil behavior of others. As you will learn, reclaiming civility is *not* about becoming a doormat. Rather, it is about how to be skillful in navigating life and thereby minimize your stress and that of your loved ones.

Heck, dare I dream big? (This is where you say, "Go for it, John.") Reclaiming civility *might* be about finding ways to bring back joy (yes, I said it, joy) to our daily lives. The choices of *who* you want to be, *how* you want to live, and *what* is most important in life are all yours to make. I hope that this book can help you recalibrate these decisions and focus more specifically on reclaiming the person that you want to be your best self.

Thankfully, all change starts with us. The journey to change isn't easy, but it's doable with a guide, which is why I wrote this book. *Rudeness Rehab* is a call to action and, ideally, a message of hope. So, sit back, fasten your seatbelts, and get ready for some immense and intense personal *change*.

We can do better. You can do better. Every moment in life is a new chance for a reset and an opportunity to start fresh.

So, let's get started.

Yours in rudeness recovery,
John

PART 1

Rude!

chapter one

Rude!
Why Should I Care About Incivility?

"What a loser. Why are we even interviewing this guy?"

"I know. What a waste of time."

A third chimed in, "Do we even bother continuing?"

My jaw dropped as I overheard this exchange—they were talking about me. Me. *I was a waste of time?*

That day, many years ago, I was interviewing for a teaching job at a local university. During a short break, I walked into the men's room. Upon seeing that the three male faculty members of the interviewing committee were all at the urinals, I had gone into the stall. They had not seen me.

Rude! The words "waste of time" rang in my ears, and my blood started to boil. Should I walk out of the stall, confront them, and stop the interview process right there?

I uttered a few expletives in my head and felt a combination of shame and anger. *Who did they think they were?* One of these faculty members had lost his license to practice therapy for unethical behavior. The other smelled like a distillery, clearly indicating that he had an issue with alcohol. My judgmental thinking kicked in and I wanted to tell them *exactly* what I thought of each of them. Would I bail?

I decided that I still had the chance to change their minds and I would show them that I was the right choice for the position in my concluding talk.

Back in front of the interviewing committee, which included other faculty members and students, I began to give my presentation—but I could not get through most of the material. The faculty member, smelling like the distillery, peppered me with questions, challenging everything that I said and disagreeing vehemently with me. After the talk, he came up to inform me that I had "poor classroom management skills" in not setting better limits with him. I was stunned, and now I felt like I was in Alice in Wonderland interacting with the Mad Hatter.

I managed to get through the rest of the day and drove home, dazed and confused. Despite all of this, I still decided that I would take the position if it was offered to me. I could then form better relationships with these professors. I figured the dysfunction was over.

I was wrong.

After the final round of interviews, I got a call. The voice on the other end told me something I'll never forget: "You don't have what it takes to teach, John. You should rethink your career." He continued in that vein until he finally paused and asked, "I don't know if you have any questions or if you want to hear more?"

I replied with the following: "Dr. Smith (not his real name), I am very grateful for your time. The purpose of this phone call was to learn if I was being considered for the position and that has been accomplished. I also have a very different experience of my ability as an instructor, but I have no need to hear anything else from you. Thank you for your time."

Meanwhile, I was thinking something along the lines of, "You can take a long walk off a short pier,"—but, fortunately, I held my tongue.

After the call, I sat perplexed and had to reach out to my support system. When I told them all what had occurred, they were stunned and angry. "Better that you did not get hired to work there."

Phew—and that was the first and last time I experienced incivility in my life.

End of story.

Not.

Whether I like it or not, incivility is a part of my everyday life. And yours, too. Rudeness, offensive behaviors, bullying—these are inescapable. Thankfully, I've learned a great deal since I walked out of that bathroom stall.

I've spent my career working with people (individually and in groups) who have experienced the negative effects of other people's behavior, whether it is more egregious behavior, like overtly abusive or bullying behavior, or uncivil behavior on the part of a boss, family member, or spouse.

While our culture in the United States has become much more aware of the concept of bullying and has put consequences in place for those who engage in this type of aggressive behavior, most of us are less aware of the more subtle but nonetheless toxic behavior that is incivility. We know incivility when others are being uncivil to us.

But do we know when we're being uncivil to others? And what can we do about it?

My job as a therapist, teacher, and consultant has been to raise people's awareness levels about these behaviors and to help them determine ways to be more effective in responding to the rude behavior of others or their own. That said, I've long felt my impact was limited in my work with individuals. Wanting to take this message outside my therapy office, I wrote this book.

What Is Incivility?

Incivility is engaging in an often unintentional but nonetheless offensive behavior that is stress-inducing in other people. For example, Porath and Pearson (2013) describe workplace incivility as "the exchange of seemingly inconsequential and inconsiderate words and deeds that violate conventional norms of workplace conduct."[4]

Some authors define incivility as a softer version of bullying. With bullying, the perpetrator is much more intentional about the behavior and there is a specific individual who is the target of the intimidation.

Incivility, meanwhile, is more likely to be inconsiderate behavior that may be directed at others but not with the intention of intimidating or silencing the other. Incivility is more likely to be about "blowing off steam" or "expressing frustration."

Incivility may simply be based on a person's low frustration tolerance. When someone is frustrated by the response (or lack thereof) of another person, they may act out of frustration in their reply. Acting out of frustration is much more likely when there is not a direct personal contact in the moment between the individuals. When there is greater social distance between ourselves and other people—such as between two anonymous people on social media—we are more likely to express our frustration without thinking about the impact on others.

I was first exposed to the concept of incivility in a presentation by Dr. Christine Porath in 2017. I resonated with a great deal of what she reviewed, and I began to see what was going on in our culture in an entirely new way.

Incivility is not limited to any one group or any one political party, but has infiltrated our interactions in person and in electronic communications (especially in social media). I've witnessed an increasing vitriol happening at the national level that has contributed to a significant divide in our country, one that I saw reflected in the individuals I saw in therapy. I wrote this book so that we may better understand ourselves and one another—and not just because it's what we "should" do.

"No mud can soil us but the mud we throw," said James Russell Lowell many years ago. When you engage in uncivil behavior or even react to this behavior in others, you experience direct consequences to your health. Incivility is one of the reasons that stress levels in our society are skyrocketing, as are rates of depression, anxiety, and substance abuse. I am passionate about helping people change their lives and reducing their health risks. Incivility and its management present us with a challenge to reduce its impact on our own health and the health of our loved ones.

> When you engage in uncivil behavior or even react to this behavior in others, you experience direct consequences to your health.

Stress, AKA How Incivility Is Killing You

Incivility affects you, whether it is your own incivility toward other people or others' behavior toward you. The general category of that impact can be defined as "stress." Stress is our natural reaction to any change in our lives.

Stress in the moment results in a "fight or flight response" that is rooted in helping us survive. Stress hormones, including adrenaline and noradrenaline, get released into the body to help us fight off the threat or outrun it. Our physiological reactions to dangers developed much earlier when our very existence as humans was under threat from potential predators, such as wild animals or other humans who were prone to violence. While these reactions helped humans survive the moment, we are now learning how the biological impact of chronic stress can shorten our lifespan.

We no longer need such levels of threat protection. Even though most of us no longer exist in environments that threaten our existence daily, our bodies still react with high degrees of intensity.

Conflicts with your spouse or being treated poorly by your boss can make stress levels surge, leading to a release of these same chemicals. Over time—if we don't manage our stress effectively or remain in environments that overwhelm our coping abilities—these reactions can wear down the body. (Even the most self-aware individuals who regularly practice effective self-care techniques can eventually be worn down if the environment is stressful enough.)

Stress can have broad-reaching impacts in the short term. Our individual reactions to stress and what may indicate that we are stressed will vary widely. However, most people will be affected on a variety of levels, including emotionally, physically, cognitively, or behaviorally. Our reaction to incivility is like a warning sign of stress.

We all experience some elements of life that will be chronic stressors, such as the challenges of every day—family, traffic, financial concerns, work pressures, and more. In other words, chronic stressors are inevitable in our lives. We don't have a choice about the presence of stressors.

We do have a choice, however, in how we manage our reactions to these stressors. And we must learn to manage them.

Poorly managed long-term stress can have a variety of negative impacts on our health, including high blood pressure, arteriosclerosis, and brain changes that can activate genetic predispositions to diseases such as depression, anxiety, or addiction. Some research also suggests that chronic stress is contributing to problems with obesity in our country, either causing us to overeat or hampering our efforts to sleep and exercise, which may have an impact on people's calorie consumption and weight. Chronic stress can increase our likelihood of cancer and cardiac problems, which shorten our lifespan and contribute to a decrease in quality of life.

The Two Ways We Experience Rudeness Today

Incivility can be divided into two separate categories: intrapersonal, which is within yourself, and interpersonal, which is between you and others. Most of us experience both on a near-daily basis.

Intrapersonal Incivility

It has often been said that we are our own worst critics. Except for people who are very bold narcissists who don't seem to have a self-critical neuron in their body, we all carry around internal "self-talk" that is a way that we think about and "talk to" ourselves.

Often our internal dialogue can be quite negative and critical of who we are or what we are doing. People sometimes think that this critical voice is necessary as a source of motivation. However, this type of internal dialogue does the exact opposite and eventually results in people being demotivated, demoralized, or depressed.

I have worked with many clients who are afraid to let go of self-judgment as a source of motivation. They struggle to believe that this type of thought process could be damaging. When I am faced with someone who remains unconvinced of this idea, I tell them the following story.

Back in the day, when my legs still tolerated the idea of running, I took on the challenge of long-distance road races. Participating in the Portland Half Marathon, we headed out of the city along scenic roadways. As we returned toward the end of this grueling challenge, we ran along a picturesque cove and could hear the roaring crowd across the water awaiting our arrival at the finish line. The trouble was, it was still a good two miles away, even though the cheers made it sound oh so close.

Now, at this point in a race, when you're pushing your limits, exhaustion is your copilot. To keep myself entertained, I had a peculiar habit of selecting a runner ahead of me and making it my mission to catch up with them. Meanwhile, I knew others were eyeing me, planning their pass.

So, there I was, scanning the field for my next prey, and I spotted this guy who seemed to be in as much agony as I was. I thought to myself, "I can definitely catch him." Slowly but surely, I closed the gap with about a mile and a quarter left to go.

Here's where the plot thickens. Out of nowhere, this guy on a bike shows up right next to Bob (or whatever his real name was; let's call him Bob). He starts cheering, "Hey, Bob! You're looking good, Bob!" I couldn't help but chuckle inside as I thought, "Buddy, none of us out here are looking remotely good. Bob and I both know it."

The bike guy kept chatting with Bob and then glanced over his shoulder at me, saying, "Well, Bob, you've got someone gaining on you. You can't let him pass you, Bob, you can't!" Now, I could hear every word, and I couldn't help but shake my head. Poor Bob tried to pick up the pace, but he was clearly struggling.

I kept my focus on the race and steadily closed in on Bob, all while the bike guy intensified his relentless commentary. "He's gaining on you, Bob. You can't let him pass you!"

My internal therapist thought, "John, maybe cut the poor guy some slack and let him finish ahead," but then my competitive side chimed in, "No, we're here to race!"

At this point, I was practically running shoulder-to-shoulder with Bob. Bob's "coach" screamed, "You can't let him pass you, Bob. *What are you? A girl?*"

At this point, I wanted to push the guy off the bike and tell him to leave Bob alone. However, I needed all my energy to finish the task at hand.

I pressed on, overtaking Bob, and eventually crossed the finish line. Now, here's the kicker: after you finish, you can look back along the course and see runners still coming toward the finish line about a third of a mile back. So, I turned around to check on Bob, and what did I see?

No Bob.

He was nowhere in sight. That relentless bike guy had managed to demoralize Bob to the point where he'd burned out and struggled to even finish.

And this is something that we can do to ourselves. This, my friends, is a prime example of what I call the notorious "judgment on a bike." We all have that internal running coach, some inner critic, that can scream at us, urging us to push harder. But often, it ends up sabotaging our performance.

As I finish telling the story, clients are usually wide-eyed with attention (like you hopefully are now). They often say something like, "Wow. I feel terrible for Bob."

I then look them directly in the eye and say, "Now think about how you are Bob and that you have a 'running coach' inside you too. *You* get to decide what you want that coach to be saying." This helps them understand the concept of internal incivility. We will explore strategies to manage our internal urges toward incivility such as "grounding" and "acceptance." Stay tuned.

Interpersonal Incivility

This type of incivility is more likely to manifest in families, work environments, and out in public. In this category, one person is directly uncivil to another. However, the level of *intensity* can vary quite significantly. It could be that a person directly insults someone else without the intention of doing so.

Family members (however you define them) can be uncivil to each other with or without intention. The more emotionally vulnerable we are due to stress, mental health issues, or physical illness, the less able we are to be skillful in our responses and interactions with others. Those with whom we live and interact are, therefore, the most likely to see us "at our worst."

The dinner table can be a time of conflict and communication breakdown. This is especially true on holidays. We often gather with family members whom we have not seen in a long time and with whom we may not have the best of relationships. This can lead to many hurt feelings and arguments, the effect of which can be felt for months or even years beyond the event.

In recent years, I have worked with people who were headed to family gatherings where others of different political persuasions or interpersonal styles would be attending. I have often successfully coached many of my clients on how to navigate holiday gatherings with Uncle Louie or Cousin Sue, who "drives them wild."

When it comes to social media and cyber incivility, there are varying levels of intention and rudeness. Some individuals take great pleasure in "calling out" others who have a different opinion and shaming them in public. Schadenfreude is a term that is defined as the feeling of taking pleasure in the misfortune or discomfort of others (from the German *schaden* for damage or harm and *freude* for joy). Our culture is increasingly driven by the "one-upmanship" or "put-downs" that are an integral part of online culture. What people fail to realize is that these behaviors affect not only the target but also the perpetrator.

When people get "fired up" to "put someone in their place," they can become more activated physiologically, which creates unnecessary stress for everyone involved. I often hear people say that they are "taking a break from social media" or "giving up social media." They may not fully realize the reason for the break, but they are making choices that often improve their stress level and overall health.

We Can Be Civil And Minimize Incivility—But How?

You might be thinking, "Yikes, incivility is all around me, even *in* me. I can't escape it and its negative impact. It is hopeless."

To that, I say, "Please, don't panic." There is, in fact, hope for you and for all of us. We can be more civil with each other, leading to better attitudes, relationships, workplaces, and family environments, and, ultimately, better health. The rest of the book, from here forward, is about the solution, a "how-to" of ways to get to greater levels of civility in your own world and strategies to limit the impact of incivility in your environment.

When I talk with clients about the ideas contained in this book, they often begin to think that I am asking them to be passive. "Oh, sure, John. You want me to just sit back and let my boss (spouse, friend, cat) walk all over me. You want me to be passive." Some think that psychologists just want everyone to join hands and sing "Kumbaya."

I want you to know something right up front. Being civil is not about being a doormat, and it is not about giving up on your needs or your beliefs. It does not mean that you never seek to improve yourself or motivate yourself toward goals. Being civil is not about swallowing your anger or never communicating your dissatisfaction with situations. It is not about "giving in" or giving up on advocating for yourself or others when in competitive situations, which is a reality of life. Dan Harris refers to this as "hiding the Zen," meaning that you can balance your mindfulness practice (and civility) with striving to achieve. He describes this to be especially applicable when you are in situations where others might take advantage of you and your "Zen" (think organizational hierarchy and people jockeying for position).[5]

Being civil is not about being a doormat.

Rather, being civil is about treating others (and yourself) with respect. It means that you respond (not react) to others with awareness. Being civil means avoiding a great deal of misunderstandings in communications with others and making it easier to clarify them when they do occur. It is about really listening to what others are saying and working to understand their perspective, even if you don't agree. Being civil means communicating your anger without *being* your anger.

Being civil is about treating others (and yourself) with respect.

The Health Benefits Of Civility

On an individual level, happiness and kindness create good feelings in us in the moment. These feelings can grow and feed upon themselves with many positive impacts, including lower stress levels, lower blood pressure, and better overall immune system function.[6] In the longer term, this leads to reductions in cardiac disease, better responses to treatment of various illnesses (including cancer), and increased life expectancy. The choices that we make individually can then have benefits not just for us but for those around us. We can reverse the disturbing public health trends noted earlier, but it begins with us individually.

So, what would it mean if we were more civil to each other? What might be some of the benefits? Let's dream big for a moment. If we were truly able to practice the art of civility with each other, we might see the following:

- lower rates of depression and anxiety
- lower rates of addiction
- lower rates of diabetes

- better overall health outcomes in general and better responses to treatments
- reduced health disparities in minority populations
- better home lives with fewer divorces
- healthier work environments with better employee retention
- increased life expectancy

I do realize that these are lofty goals and likely ones that we are not going to accomplish quickly or easily. However, they are attainable. They start with each of us individually and how we choose to be in our lives with others. Remember, it is not just good for others in your life or the greater humanity. These concepts are good for you and will create a life in which you can live longer and healthier.[7]

What You Will Get From This Book

Hopefully, you now have a better understanding of what incivility means, and you are convinced that it is important to reduce the impact of rudeness on your life. But you have a very busy life and are very aware of how precious time is. Why should you bother with a "rudeness rehab"? As a result of taking time to read the chapters ahead, you will be able to do the following:

- Identify how incivility affects you emotionally, with an emphasis on anger.
- Describe how chronic anger held over the long term becomes hostility and the impact of this on your health.
- Define numerous terms related to stress.
- Discuss how stress, especially chronic stress, can create risks for negative health outcomes for you.

- Separate the internal experience of a feeling from the external behavior that you express related to the feeling.
- Implement skills to manage your internal reactions to your own behavior and that of others.
- Employ strategies to respond skillfully to directly experiencing or witnessing incivility on the part of others.
- Create a self-care plan to maximize your resilience.
- Consider the next steps that you can take to learn more about incivility or to become increasingly more skillful in managing incivility rooted in yourself or others.

The Least You Need To Know

- Our culture is aware of the destructive effects of overt bullying but less conscious of the negative impact of rudeness and incivility.
- Incivility is behavior that is often unintentional but nonetheless offensive and induces stress in other people. It is about "blowing off steam" at other people (or oneself) as an expression of frustration.
- Stress associated with uncivil behavior can create health risks and illness in both the short and long term.
- Incivility can be expressed *intrapersonally* (internal) or *interpersonally* (with others).
- If individuals reclaim a greater focus on awareness and civility, they will experience greater health and wellness for themselves and those with whom they interact.

chapter two

The Incivility Within Us:
We Have Seen The Enemy And It Is Us

The first time it happened, I thought maybe I was getting forgetful. Then it happened a second and third time. I knew something was wrong.

Every day I brought my lunch to work. I would keep it in the community refrigerator and get it when it was time to eat.

Then, one day, I went to the refrigerator as usual but found my lunch was gone. *Whaaaaaat? Where could it be?* I looked everywhere, but there was no evidence of my missing lunch. As I ate at a shop around the corner, I thought the incident was just my oversight or a one-off mistake.

Until it happened again. And again. It was becoming a regular occurrence, not simply a case of what my Aunt Janet called "CRS" (Can't Remember Stuff; she had a different third word for this acronym, but you get my point).

Given that our office had only ten clinicians, I thought that identifying the "perp" would be an easy enough task. I put myself in the mindset of the Hardy Boys and set about to solve this "crime."

After interrogating the clinicians in the office, I was down to two people, a husband and a wife. At this point, I figured out who it was and confronted him about this situation. He was immediately apologetic.

I had assumed that the theft was intentional. But in fact, I heard a different story than I'd imagined.

The clinician and his wife had a young family that they were trying to raise together while both working full-time. In the chaos that was their life, the husband had become confused about the lunches his wife packed for him. He promised to be more careful in the future.

After that conversation, I was never missing another lunch. I was also aware that the incivility we perceive usually has origins unrelated to us.

As we learn when we are young, "Don't ever assume because it makes . . . . "

Incivility In *Others*

Few people (if any) get up in the morning and choose rudeness. People are not actively thinking, "How can I go about irritating my fellow human beings today? How many ways can I get under people's skin?" Most people are well-intentioned when it comes to interactions with others. Yet, despite best efforts, behavior can slip into incivility and cause mild irritation, frustration, or major aggravation to other people. What is behind this lack of civility in others?

In our clinic, our front office manager (and angel), Carla, sometimes deals with clients "melting down" in sadness or anger about their lack of insurance coverage. She is the "front lines" of the insurance industry and sometimes the "bearer of bad news" about an employer's insurance plan that someone may not have really understood. Carla has a sign on the side of her window on the inside that is visible to staff as they approach the window to talk to a client. It is a saying often attributed to Reverend John Watson that reminds us of the importance of compassion: "Be kind. Everyone you meet is carrying a heavy burden."

It is very easy for us to personalize the behavior of others in a situation and assume that their rude actions and reactions are all about us. We forget that this person had a full life experience prior to this interaction and that many things had happened to them outside of this contact with us.

In fact, there are various factors that might influence someone's behavior. The following variables should be considered.

Stress

Life is inherently stressful. We all deal with stressors in daily life (traffic, weather, work, finances, and family responsibilities). In addition, we can experience more severe stressors, such as significant health challenges, intense relationship conflicts, or the sudden loss of a job. The more stress we experience (and the more intense it is), the more likely we are to have our behavior influenced by it.

When people are stressed, they are more likely to engage in their worst behaviors and to be short or critical with others.

Genetics

We are all wired differently physiologically. This internal wiring is based on genetics that have been handed down through our families, which is based both on family physiology as well as family experiences. Yes, genes in families are shaped by the experiences of our elders.[8]

Research examining the genes of Holocaust survivors has identified ways that their genetic codes were shaped by this experience and led their offspring to have greater reactivity to stress.[9,10] While the exact genetic code is not changed, the ways that the code is expressed are influenced by a process known as epigenetics. This could result in people being more likely to react to stress, to react more intensely when they do, and to take longer to calm down. During this period of increased reactivity, people will not be at their best and will likely engage in their worst behaviors.

Lack Of Emotional Intelligence

Emotional intelligence includes our ability to be aware of and regulate our own emotions, as well as being empathic with how others may feel and understand what may help them. Emotional intelligence is something that we may develop in life due to parenting or experiences. Genetics may also predispose us to these behaviors or lack thereof. If we don't have these skills, we are more likely to become merged with our feelings and be our feelings as opposed to having them. Acting directly based on emotion with little to no self-reflection often leads people to uncivil and inconsiderate behaviors at best or aggressive and destructive behaviors at worst.

Mental Health Concerns

Each year, about one in every five adults in America will experience some mental health issues, with one in every twenty experiencing serious mental health symptoms. Over the course of a lifetime, about 50 percent of Americans will experience a mental health disorder. These mental health symptoms have been taught in psychology departments under the name "abnormal psychology." But if 50 percent of us will experience some symptoms at some point in our lifetimes, then how "abnormal" are they anyway?[10,11] When people are experiencing a mental health crisis of some kind, their thinking will be affected, sometimes in subtle ways and sometimes in very serious ways. Regardless of the intensity of the impact, mental health symptoms can cause the person to distort their own behavior or the behavior of others. These distortions can lead the person to be more reactive or uncivil in ways that shock or surprise us.[11]

However, we may have no idea that the person is experiencing symptoms. Unlike a broken arm or leg, depression or anxiety can affect a person in ways that are not visible. We are then surprised or angered by their behavior without realizing the source.

Substance Abuse

The National Institute on Alcohol Abuse and Alcoholism reported that about 84 percent of adults ages eighteen and older indicated that they had used alcohol at some point in their lifetime. This means that most Americans have at least tried alcohol.[12] This does not mean that all these Americans are alcoholics. However, as I say to clients, "Someone may not have a problem with alcohol, but alcohol can still be a problem." My message here is that someone may not have a diagnosable alcohol issue, but their use can still create issues for the person and their loved ones. This is also true for the use of marijuana and other substances that may be used recreationally (including caffeine and nicotine).[13,14]

Alcohol is a depressant, which means that it slows activity in our bodies, leaving us sedated and perhaps even giddy. Some would put marijuana in the same category. Caffeine and nicotine are stimulants that can leave us over-activated and more "wound up" physiologically. Whether someone is "wound down" or "wound up," they can have reduced inhibitions and be more likely to say/do things that they would not normally do. These people are more likely to also distort situations and fail to recognize the impact of their behavior.

Years ago, I used to show my students a video about a man going to a company holiday party. You first see the party from the point of view of the individual who was drinking. He believes that he is the life of the party and has been able to successfully joke with his boss and the boss's wife while his own wife looks on with happiness. You then see the same scenario from the viewpoint of others, wherein the man is so intoxicated that he is staggering around the party. He interacts with his boss and the boss's wife in ways that are offensive and demeaning. His wife looks on in horror.

Although this extreme example illustrates the impact of addiction, this same situation can occur in a less intense but nonetheless still negative way that alienates/offends others. Substance use at any level can affect individuals and be the source of uncivil behaviors.

Personality

Personality styles are variables that will influence the way someone communicates. Some people are very person-focused, while other people are very problem-focused. There are advantages to both styles, and there is no one better. Person-focused individuals can be very sensitive and caring with others but have trouble when they need to address problem behaviors in others. Problem-focused people are great at seeing a task through to completion, but they can be perceived as insensitive, rude, or blunt when they are saying "what needs to be said."

A person's level of interpersonal sensitivity will lead them to be more attuned or less attuned to the impact of their behavior on others. This can lead the less attuned in our ranks to be oblivious to the hurt feelings and irritations they leave in their wake.

Environment

The environment strongly influences our behaviors, stress levels, and interpretation of others' behaviors. Some environments are just more intensely stressful. Think about healthcare environments, including hospitals, clinics, and even pharmacies. People may be stressed by their physical/emotional concerns that are causing them to visit the facility or by the bills that they must pay for these services.

I remember my former boss, Ann, insisting that our team create a healthy interpersonal environment in our work as a partial hospital team at a psychiatric hospital. She noted how important it was that we treated each other with respect and caring, both for our benefit (in wanting to come to work) as well as the benefit of our patients. She said that the environment we maintained within the staff would trickle down and influence how patients felt in the program. I have never forgotten this wisdom, and our mental health practice has always sought to create harmony in the staff. I think that it translates into people feeling good about coming to our office and being more likely to get and give respect.

When people don't pay attention to the dynamics between individuals, places can devolve into cynical and hostile environments. This can happen in workplaces, professional organizations, or even families. Unfortunately, uncivil and toxic workplaces generate increasing levels of these behaviors, leading to irritation and anger on the part of workers and, therefore, customers.

Previous Experience

When I went to college, the theories at the time divided nature and nurture quite cleanly and clearly. Nature was the genetics we were born with, and nurture was our experience after birth. There was no overlap. In addition, it was thought that we had a certain number of brain cells that were slowly dying off over our lifetime and that the brain did not have the ability to regenerate lost cells or cell functions. I remember thinking, "I will probably have about seven brain cells left after all these college parties. I better protect those seven cells carefully for the rest of my life, as this is all I will have left."

We now know so much more about the brain, including that it can regenerate lost functions and create new cells based on experiences. Neural pathways that are reinforced by experience get strengthened, and neural pathways with little to no stimulation weaken and eventually die off. In short, our experiences shape our brains and may make us more likely to act in certain ways. Our behavior can, therefore, be predisposed to be more or less compassionate, depending upon our experiences and the strength of neural connections. Sometimes, the people that we think would be more compassionate turn out to be less compassionate. Let me give you an example.

Quitting smoking is not an easy task. Although almost 70 percent of smokers in the United States want to quit, only about 7.5 percent will be ultimately successful in doing so each year.[15] As you can see, this translates into an actual quit rate of approximately 10 percent. One would assume that this 10 percent of former smokers would be incredibly compassionate with their former smoke break buddies. However, that is often not the case.

Former smokers are often the most antismoking of people. They can think, "I did it, so you should be able to do so too." They can be very judgmental of those still smoking and sometimes are the most strident in pushing for limits on smoking areas. This can lead to uncivil behaviors on the part of the former smokers. This same dynamic translates into various substance and behavior patterns (e.g., those who have lost weight and those who have successfully left a bad relationship).

Culture

Culture plays a significant role in how prevalent these "uncivil" behaviors may be. Culture also influences what is perceived as civil or uncivil.

For example, I remember landing in Rome after an overnight flight on which I had not slept. As I staggered, sleep-deprived, in search of a coffee before my next flight, I remember the intensity of sights and sounds around me. I do not speak Italian, but I was reacting to the nonverbal elements of the communication. Everyone seemed to be *yelling* at each other and waving their hands in what I perceived as aggressive gestures as they talked. What I finally realized as I got coffee into my system and began to be slightly more alert was that I was seeing the *norm* of their communications. They were simply engaged in normal everyday interactions. These types of behaviors are quite normal for people from Mediterranean cultures, whereas

The Incivility Within Us: We Have Seen The Enemy And It Is Us | 31

"my people" (of northern European background) are much more subdued in our interactions.

Culture and language interact to influence the ways that people interpret their environment. This can also affect their view of what is and is not uncivil. There is a psychological theory called "Whorf's Linguistic Relativity Hypothesis." In short, this theory says that language strongly influences the ways that speakers of that language label and perceive their world.[16]

For example, some cultures are known for being very direct. Germans are a great example. I was first exposed to this when I began to study the German language years ago. I met a new friend named Guenther from Germany while he was traveling in the United States before his required service in the German army. After he returned home, we stayed in touch via letters and phone calls (yes, these were the days before all the technology we have now). He invited me to visit him and his family, which I did in April 1990, just after the wall between East and West Berlin came down. It was an amazing visit and provided me with important insights. Although my friend was fluent in English, his parents did not speak a word of it. Therefore, I relied on my friend as an interpreter or on using gestures and sounds to get my point across. I became highly motivated to learn how to speak directly with them on my next visit, and I immediately enrolled in a German class when I returned to the United States.

Early in my learning, the instructor had us read a fairy tale entitled "*Das Rotkäpchen*" (in English, "Little Red Riding Hood"). I was shocked to read how much more graphic the story was in German than in the American (English) version. However, the most illustrative component was how the story ended. In English, our fairy tales end with, "And they lived happily ever after." In the German version, the ending is quite different: "*Und wenn Sie nicht gestorben sind, dann leben Sie noch heute.*" Literal translation: "And if they are not dead, they are still alive today."

This one-sentence difference captures my experience of how different Americans and Germans are in their directness. I have seen more real-world examples of this. A good friend of mine had one grandmother in the United States and one in Germany. She once told me, "I say things to my grandmother in Germany (in German) that I would never say to my grandmother in the United States (in English)." I asked for an example. She immediately replied with the following sentence that she would often say to her grandmother in Germany (in German): "Grandmother, I hope that you are still alive the next time that I visit." For those of us in the United States, *can you imagine saying this to your grandmother?* I would think not.

More recently, I met another friend in Germany, also named Guenter (but with no "h"). I am known for making quite merry during the Christmas holidays, and I enjoy sending gifts to friends from a distance and overseas. I packed up a gift box and sent it to Guenter and his wife. When I inquired later if they had received the gift, he indicated that he had, and he expressed gratitude for the thoughtfulness. I am from Portland, Maine, where we are known for many things, including the coffee. I had proudly sent them a pound of coffee freshly produced here in Maine. I, therefore, went on and asked, "Did you like the coffee?" There is an old expression that is something like, "Don't ask a question if you don't want to know the answer." He replied with German directness and honesty (in German): "No, I don't like that coffee. I gave it to my parents, who don't care if coffee is of high quality." I remember being quite taken aback at this exchange. We laugh about this to this day. He and his wife chuckle at how *indirect* I am when speaking German despite my increasing fluency in the language. On the other hand, Germans can be perceived as rude when speaking English with the directness that is customary in German.

In short, when it comes to incivility, culture matters.

Incivility In *Ourselves*

If you ask most people about incivility, they will immediately begin to talk about their concerns about other people. Others are the source of uncivil behaviors and rudeness. "The problem couldn't be me, right?"

If we are going to talk about the problem of incivility, we must be willing to examine our own lives and behaviors. When clients talk about issues in their relationships, they often begin to recount how their spouse/partner/mother/father/brother/sister/child needs to change their behavior.

Clients are always a bit taken aback when I ask, "And what is your role in contributing to this problem?" (Secret: I learned this from my doctoral advisor, Linda Forrest. I would recount the latest problem I had with another faculty member or peer and complain bitterly about how much of a pain in the you-know-what they were. She would then smile, lean forward in her chair, look directly into my eyes, and say, "And how are you part of the problem? What part of this is about you?" I never liked that part. However, I remember growing from these conversations. So, I am now encouraging the same in you.)

> Clients are always a bit taken aback when I ask, "And what is your role in contributing to this problem?"

All the things I have identified as sources of incivility in others can also apply to us. In addition, other intrapersonal variables can influence our approach to interactions and make us more likely to be uncivil.

Negativity Bias

As humans, we are genetically programmed to be attuned to threats, whether physical or emotional. This means that we are constantly scanning the environment to be on the lookout for anything that could cause us harm. This leads to a psychological principle called the "negativity bias."

The negativity bias can have a profound impact on the way that we perceive and react to the world. It can mean we pay more attention to negative information, learn more from negative events, and make decisions more often based on negative facts. This can lead us to be primed to expect negative behaviors in others to be more likely than positive ones. We are, therefore, more likely to view the behaviors of others as intentionally uncivil (as opposed to unintentional) and will respond accordingly.[17]

The Fundamental Attribution Error And The Self-Serving Bias

These biases are more specifically related to how we view the behavior of others as well as our own. *The fundamental attribution error* means that we are more likely to view the behavior of others as representative of their disposition as opposed to their environment. We overestimate the impact of personality and underestimate the impact of situation. This means that we are more likely to judge others as mean, bad, or wrong and act out of these assumptions.

Naturally, when we look at interpersonal situations, we recognize that *we are special* and *different*, which means that there are different rules when it comes to understanding our own situation. *The self-serving bias* means that we attribute our successes to internal factors and our problems and failures to external factors. When we have issues or are unsuccessful, we will more than likely see others as the cause of this, even when it is not the case. I hear this all the time on campus, even when it comes to my classes. "I earned an A in O'Brien's class" versus "O'Brien gave me a C." These interpretations can lead us to act out our frustration or a sense of being treated unjustly by others with uncivil responses.

Self-Judgment

As I mentioned previously, people struggle with various levels of self-criticism and judgment. We will explore this concept at different points throughout the book. People can get quite caught up in this thought process and even be impaired or paralyzed by this negative thinking. This leads people to be relentless in their pursuit of perfection in whatever they do and, therefore, never be satisfied with what they do: "I could always improve my performance."

This insatiability can also be applied to others. People with high standards for themselves may expect the same of others and be disrespectful or uncivil when those individuals do not meet their standards. We often are unaware that our expectations are unreasonable or that our frustrations are viewed as disrespectful.

Dislike Of Self That Is Expressed Indirectly

As the old saying goes, "We have met the enemy, and it is us." We all have things we do not like about ourselves, past or present. Sometimes, we are aware of those parts of ourselves that we do not like. Sometimes, we are not consciously aware of what those facets may be. Nevertheless, this dislike of parts of us can lead to a very complex psychological process known as "projective identification."

Projective identification occurs when we believe we see in others some aspects of ourselves that we do not like and start to treat them accordingly. Ultimately, it can lead the "other" to start to believe that they possess that quality. For example, if you tend toward rigid thinking and a narrow sense of right and wrong, you may believe what you see and then express dislike of that in other people. "You need to relax more," you may say to that person. You may also engage in uncivil behavior toward that person because of how you view them.

Peace Begins Inside

When I talk with people about incivility, they are very quick to identify it in others, in social media, and in so many aspects of our culture. They are less likely to want to consider ways that they, too, contribute to this problem. And yet, as Dorothy Firman noted, "Peace begins not only at home, but it begins [also] inside."[18]

We have examined many factors that can contribute to incivility in ourselves and in others. This list is not exhaustive, but my hope is that it illustrates to you that there are many causes for our own behavior and the behavior of others. Many of these same variables can lead people to experience problems with anger.

In the next chapter, we will focus on anger and its impacts on people, whether they externalize or internalize it. However, in the spirit of offering hope to you, the reader, we will next discuss skills of awareness and mindfulness and how these strategies offer us the chance to not *react emotionally* to others but rather to *respond effectively*.

The Least You Need To Know

- Few people, when they leave their homes and head out into the world to interact with others, desire to be irritating or uncivil to others.

- Many factors contribute to people's behavior and uncivil actions toward others.

- Understanding variables that underlie other people's behavior does not excuse actions that are uncivil but rather can help us put this behavior in context.

- We can be uncivil toward ourselves for a variety of reasons, many of which are rooted in the experience of being human.

- The only way to change our society is by changing ourselves. "Peace begins at home."

chapter three

Anger And Our Response:
Sure, "Everyone Else" Has A Problem

Y*ep–he's sticking up his middle finger, just for me*, I realized.

I was driving back late on a Friday afternoon after teaching in Augusta, Maine. The drive was just under an hour, and it had been a long week. I was exhausted, and I looked forward to arriving home, putting my feet up, and enjoying an "adult beverage."

About halfway home, I was driving past an onramp where other cars could merge onto the interstate. There was one car that I saw attempting to enter, and I dutifully moved to the left lane to allow this driver to easily access the roadway. This is just a courteous driving habit, and I do this so often, nearly every time I drive, that you would think that it is not even worth mentioning—except on this day when this driver was different.

I noticed that the car entering the highway seemed to be traveling at an increasingly rapid speed, far beyond what is typical for "merging with traffic on the highway." As the car entered, the driver decided to immediately transition into the high-speed left lane where I was now traveling. In one motion, he accelerated and swung directly in front of me, forcing me to slam on my brakes so that I did not hit him.

As if this was not enough of an affront, the driver had his hand out the window with his fist visible in the air, holding up his middle finger. He sped off.

Lovely.

This was a Friday afternoon when my resources were already depleted. I was both speechless and rageful at what had just occurred. It took me some time to calm myself down on the remaining journey home. I was just glad that I did not have to see this person ever again. I had a taste of his anger and "caught it" for a few minutes. He was living in this anger and spreading it through the world, leaving anyone in his wake the worse for having contact with him.

> I had a taste of his anger and "caught it" for a few minutes. He was living in this anger and spreading it through the world . . .

I'm Angry Therefore I'm Uncivil

People often say that "anger is the problem" with our society. I am only willing to partially agree. Anger is not the primary problem. Anger is an emotion that has its purpose in our lives. Anger signals that we feel threatened or as if our rights have been violated. Anger is a feeling happening internally. Aggression is an external behavior and is the manifestation of anger. Anger is not the problem. Aggression and what we do with our anger are the problem.

Unfortunately, many people have limited awareness of their anger or how to manage it. This can lead to people going through life with poorly managed angry reactions to others or situations they encounter. This unmanaged anger results in a variety of health impacts, depending upon the nature and intensity of this emotion. Poorly managed anger includes two forms: "exploding out" and "exploding in."

Exploding Out

We tend to think of "exploding out" as the manifestation of anger problems. This occurs when people become visibly angry or rageful. As anger levels increase, people become less able to regulate their behaviors and have less access to areas of the brain in charge of problem-solving skills and controlling their behavior. Eventually, people can "blackout" in episodes of intense rage where they lose touch with what they are doing and their surroundings. When people do subsequently calm down, they may have little to no awareness of what just happened.

When people "explode out" in this way, they put excessive stress on themselves and their bodies (as well as others around them). Blood pressure levels increase, and the cardiovascular system comes under increased stress. There are some data to suggest that blood pressure levels remain high up to two hours after the person first becomes angry. This can lead to stroke, blood clots, or even bleeding in the brain, especially for those who have not been good at monitoring their own health with regular visits to their physician.

Exploding In

I have worked clinically with many people over the years who have exhibited chronic anger problems of exploding out (sometimes at me, imagine my joy). However, there is another and less well-known category of those with anger problems: those who "explode in."

In my personal experience, these individuals are more likely to be women. Unfortunately, our society in the United States has given women the inaccurate message that they are not supposed to be angry. Those women who do exhibit anger are much more likely to be labeled as "out of control" (or with other terms, one of which rhymes with "witch") as compared to their male counterparts. "Being angry is not ladylike." (I am not saying this, but rather noting that this is a message that many women get.)

There is another category of people likely to explode in: those who have experienced abuse of some kind, especially as children. These individuals do not feel safe expressing their real feelings. They learn to "swallow their anger" and simply push it down inside, thinking that they can forget it and get beyond it. However, unexpressed emotion will find a way to express itself, and anger is no exception. The anger may come out in physiological symptoms (such as an impaired immune system, blood pressure problems, or cardiac issues) or psychiatric symptoms that include anxiety, depression, or chronic suicidal behavior.[19]

I have worked clinically with those who engage in chronic self-harming behaviors, including cutting or burning oneself. Many of these clients had also attempted to kill themselves and lived with chronic thoughts of death. In working with them, I would encourage them to think about the role of anger in their symptoms.

I think of one client with whom I have worked for many years. She was often in the emergency room, having engaged in an attempt at suicide or having urges to do so. She lived with high levels of suicidal thinking every day. When we began to focus on helping to reduce these symptoms, I would talk with her about her anger.

She was flat in her affect and would say, "I don't feel angry. I don't understand what you are talking about." We laugh about this now, and she tells me I am responsible for helping her "find her anger." She says, "Thanks a lot, John." I reminded her that finding her anger and ways to express it more directly reduced her symptoms and her need for psychiatric hospitalization. Over time, she has been less reliant on the local psychiatric services and on me and is better able to regulate her behavior.

There is a special form of anger in those who carry it around all the time: hostility. Hostility is defined by the Merriam-Webster online dictionary as "deep seated, usually mutual ill will" or "hostile action."[20] I remember seeing a bumper sticker years ago on a car near me on the highway. It read, "Your hate becomes you." There was an intended sarcastic double meaning to this message as in, "It looks good on you." However, the primary meaning was important. Live in a state of chronic anger or hate, and it will affect you physically.

Over the years, research has documented the extremely negative effects of living in anger. Those who exist in a state of hate are much more likely to have coronary artery disease and to die earlier of several causes. A hostile approach to the world not only creates greater health challenges but also complicates the efforts of others to help the individual. This means that the quality of the health care this person receives can be compromised and, therefore, lead to poorer outcomes of treatment.[21]

Hostility makes people more likely to react with greater intensity to environmental stressors. Hostile people are more prone to episodes of extreme anger in daily life, especially due to interpersonal interactions, and are more likely to engage in unhealthy forms of coping, such as smoking cigarettes and using alcohol excessively. Living with hostility kills us.

Now, consider incivility's role as one of those provocations in everyday life. Uncivil episodes can create reactions varying from mild irritation to extreme rage, depending upon the circumstances and the individual's coping mechanisms (or lack thereof). Incivility, whether ours or that of another, can be the driver of anger that results in chronic health impacts and can shorten our lifespan.

Clients I have worked with who have lost a significant amount of weight to get healthier often tell me the same thing: "I never realized the impact that the extra weight was having." They tell me of less joint pain, less back pain, and less difficulty moving through the world. They never would have known how things could be different without losing weight.

The same is true when it comes to the burdens of being uncivil—anger, depression, anxiety, and so much more. People do not realize the impact that incivility is having on them until they reduce it by being aware of it. They then discover how much easier it is to "move through the world" when they are aware of being more civil, internally and externally.

> **Awareness**
> According to the Merriam-Webster dictionary, awareness is "knowledge and understanding that something is happening or exists."[22] This means that we bring the existence of something, internal or external, into our focus. Awareness is the opposite of denial or being oblivious to the existence of something. Before we explore these concepts further, let me give you an example of why awareness is important.

The Case Of Barry

Barry was a gay man in his late forties who came to treatment due to depression and anxiety. One of Barry's major stressors was his relationship with his husband, Sam. Barry and Sam had been married for six years, and Barry lamented in our meetings about how critical and insensitive Sam could be. In taking a history with Barry, he mentioned how he grew up in a conservative religious family with high standards and "expectations of perfection." This would be an important variable in understanding what happened next.

In one of our sessions, Barry was describing the latest injustice that Sam had committed in being critical of him. I offered an insight into what might be happening, and Barry scoffed at my idea. "No, John. That is not it at all." He rolled his eyes with derision and continued with his story.

I interrupted Barry and asked him to reflect on what had just happened. He looked at me as if I had suddenly switched to speaking a different language. I asked him to reflect on what he had said to me but, more importantly, how he had said it to me. Barry was still not clear on my point. I reflected to him how he had been dismissive both verbally and nonverbally of what I said. I noted that perhaps these dynamics might be happening with Sam and contributing to their conflicts.

There are times when I offer feedback to clients, leading their eyes to grow wide with amazement and leading to a smile of acknowledgment. They are so very grateful for my support and appreciate my insights. This was not one of those times.

Barry was immediately defensive and continued to scoff at what I said. I thought that he might storm out (as has happened with clients at times, most of whom eventually returned). To Barry's credit, he stayed and struggled with me. We ended our meeting on a tense note with the promise of continuing the discussion the next week.

When Barry returned, he was in a very different mood. He had taken the time to reflect on what had happened and realized that he had, in fact, been dismissive. This led him to identify "the angry guy" inside of him, who could be quite disruptive and uncivil at times. Over time, Barry was able to reflect on how his verbal and nonverbal behavior was contributing to his relationship difficulties.

Self-Awareness

When it comes to awareness of incivility and how to change it in your environment, you must start with yourself first. I know, I know: You think it would be much easier if everyone else in your world changed their uncivil behaviors. Gosh, that would be great. Unfortunately, you cannot depend upon this; ultimately, we can only change ourselves.

So, when it comes to dealing with and changing incivility in your life, you can think of it like getting on a plane and hearing the safety procedures outlined. "Oxygen masks will drop from overhead. Please get your own masks on before helping children or others." You need to begin with yourself and grow in your own self-awareness. Once you have reflected on yourself and your own behavior, you will be better able to respond to the behavior of others.

One useful concept regarding self-awareness is the Johari window. Although this sounds quite mystical, the Johari window was created by two men. (Can you guess their names? You are correct: Joe and Harry.) Joseph Luft and Harrington Ingham created this model of self-knowledge in 1955. The Johari window was developed as a self-help tool for understanding and growing self-awareness.[23]

	known to self	unknown to self
known to others	**Open Self** Information about you that both you, and others know.	**Blind Self** Information about you that others know, but you do not.
unknown to others	**Hidden Self** Information about you that you know, but others do not.	**Unknown Self** Information about you that neither you, nor others know.

As you can see in the model, there are four quadrants that relate to information about yourself and how you, as well as others, see you:

- Open: information known to you and others
- Hidden: information you know, but others do not
- Blind: information others know, but you do not
- Unknown: information not yet understood by you or others

Your goal in the model is to move the center line to the right by constantly growing in your understanding of yourself and your impact on others.

Being attuned to ourselves and our lives helps us to then grow our understanding of our unique situation. I often hear people who have successfully managed a situation tell others who are experiencing the same circumstance: "I know exactly what you are feeling." I try to gently point out to my clients that this is not true (if they tell me they are saying these things to family or friends). No one knows exactly what you are thinking or feeling except you. No one knows the intricacies of your circumstance except you.

Reaction Versus Response

However, there are other reasons that awareness can help. Many people go through life in "reaction" mode wherein they act out of their emotions without taking time to stop and reflect on their situation. Being attuned to our experience helps us to understand more of our internal reactions to situations. You can get clear about what you are thinking and feeling. What is the difference between reacting and responding? Let's turn to some definitions.

A reaction is "a bodily response to or activity aroused by a stimulus," according to the Merriam-Webster dictionary.[24] We react out of our brain's limbic system, where a structure known as the amygdala oversees our responses to the environment and focuses on helping us survive threats. When our ancestors were faced with a threat, they did not take time to go to a support group or read a self-help book to determine a course of action. Their existence was threatened now. The greater the threat was to them, the greater the role of emotion in shaping their response. In highly threatening situations, their limited ability for thought was hijacked completely by emotion, and they acted more out of impulse to get through the immediate threat.

Those who did survive the threats developed stronger links in their neural networks to these survival instincts.

Guess what? These people are ancient relatives of you and me. We inherited these same tendencies via neurobiology and can easily have our functioning hijacked in stressful situations by emotions. The greater the threat that we experience, the greater our emotions will be, and the harder it will then be to "keep our wits about us." Furthermore, our life experiences shape our brains, including structures like the amygdala, which can become even more reactive due to experiencing trauma. Traumatic experiences can, therefore, make us more likely to react and to react more intensely.

These overactive responses of the amygdala still tend to overwhelm our cognitive abilities, even though our brains have much more capacity for self-reflection than those of our ancient relatives. Your more intense emotional responses will make you less likely to be thoughtful in how you respond to others. This makes you less likely to be skillful in interpersonal situations. Reactive behavior most often fuels conflict and disagreements. I always tell clients that if they are reactive, others in the situation can focus on them, and that their reaction is inappropriate instead of addressing the real problem. Reactivity becomes a distraction and can lead others to get distracted and see you as the real issue.

The Merriam-Webster dictionary indicates that to respond is to "make an answer."[25] Embedded in this definition is that we take time to create our answer to a situation. Responding to something is not emotionless and robotic; it involves greater use of our full cognitive powers. When we respond to something, we are more grounded and skillful. We have more perspective and can tune into both our thoughts and our emotions. We have emotions and thoughts as opposed to being our emotions and simply believing our emotionally-based thinking to be true.

Why is it important to be attuned to our thoughts and emotions? As we determine how to best respond to others, both our thoughts and emotions are important sources of information. Once we name our thoughts and feelings, we have more of a sense of control over them. We can consider whether we are focused on true facts or on feelings that we think are facts. We can gain perspective and then consider the most effective way to handle the situation. Labeling our experience allows us some time to pause and reflect, even if just for a millisecond. Awareness, in this sense, gives us more choices about what we do.

So, hopefully, you are now more aware of why awareness is important as a foundation for understanding and behavior change. We can't solve problems that we don't know exist, and we cannot effectively solve problems unless we have all the information. Awareness can give us both.

Now, pay attention here because you are at a choice point in reading this book. This book can be your opportunity to create greater levels of awareness and get on the path to rudeness recovery. Hopefully, I have helped you be more aware of incivility in your life. Now, you are the lightbulb. Do you want to change? That is up to you.

Reclaiming Civility In An Angry And Stressed-Out World

In the first part of the book, my intent has been to raise your awareness about rudeness and incivility. Hopefully, you now understand that there are many variables that can contribute to uncivil behavior on the part of others, some of which are beyond someone's control (think genetics and environmental stress) and others that may be rooted in personality (think being too direct) or in lack of self-awareness or skills.

> In the first part of the book, my intent has been to raise your awareness about rudeness and incivility.

These factors do not mean that the perpetrator of incivility is not responsible for their behavior. Rather, these variables can help you understand the root causes contributing to this person's uncivil behavior (or your own?) and that it may not be intentional.

So, what now? I'm glad that you asked.

What follows is about what to do about incivility, whether your own or another person's behavior.

In the pages ahead, I will teach you skills that have helped me to grow my awareness of my own uncivil behavior and how to change it, as well as ways to effectively respond to rude behaviors on the part of others. These are skills that I can attest to personally using and ones that I have taught to hundreds of clients over the years. I have found that they have helped to reduce my clients' stressful reactions (and mine) to interpersonal stress and, therefore, improved their potential for a happier and healthier life.

Part 2 describes intrapersonal skills, the techniques that will help you to change your internal reactions to incivility and reduce your reactivity. By using these strategies and reducing the intensity of your reactions, you can be more effective at responding to others. In addition, you can lower the stress on your nervous system and risks for your long-term health.

Part 3 provides interpersonal skills and strategies that you can implement to respond clearly and directly to others. People sometimes get the idea that being civil means being passive and allowing others to "run roughshod" over you. As you will see, these skills can help us to stand up for ourselves and protect ourselves in a way that no one is treated poorly.

The end of the book will provide you with what I have labeled a "Call to Action." Rudeness and incivility are everywhere and seemingly on the rise. We can do better as a society, but each of us can only be responsible for making the change to ourselves.

Are you ready? If so, I invite you to turn the page (literally) on your old behavior and let the change begin.

The Least You Need To Know

- Anger is an emotion (internal) that is a natural part of being human and is only a potential problem for the individual experiencing it. Aggression is the behavioral expression of anger that is directed toward others and is more the source of problems in our society.

- Awareness and, more specifically, mindfulness can help us to let go of judgments of ourselves and others so that we can deal more directly with the reality of "what is" in our lives.

- Changing behavior is not easy or simple; rather, it is a process that has awareness at its core.

- Self-awareness is something that we can develop over time if we choose to do so.

- Developing skills of self-awareness and mindfulness can help us to respond to others more effectively as opposed to reacting emotionally.

PART 2

Reclaiming Civility Within Ourselves

chapter four

Breathing:
Even More Essential Than We Realize

Quite often, when clients first come to treatment for stress and anxiety, I notice some similar patterns. Many have a very stiff body posture and seem disconnected from their bodies. I always ask people about their use of caffeine or nicotine and usually learn that they use large amounts of these substances. However, one of the things I notice most often is that these people are shallow breathers or are holding their breath for long periods of time. I point this out to them when the time is right to help them begin to recognize that there is a connection between their body awareness or lack thereof and their symptoms of anxiety and stress. And oftentimes, the experience of incivility, especially directed at self, is underneath one's anxious presentation.

> I point this out to them when the time is right to help them begin to recognize that there is a connection between their body awareness or lack thereof and their symptoms of anxiety and stress.

One of the other common patterns that I see is that many of these individuals will ask me for help in eliminating all their anxiety. I think I startle them when I tell them that I'm not going to do that and, in fact, it is not in their best interest. I have received many quizzical looks over the years when I answer them in this way, but let me explain.

All emotions and physical sensations can have a purpose in life. Anxiety, whether we think about it as an emotion or as a physical sensation, also has a purpose. Anxiety can help us understand that something about a particular situation is not right or comfortable. It can also help us realize that our *safety* is compromised in the moment. However, there is an even more important role that anxiety plays in everyday life: performance.

Anxiety at moderate levels helps us to perform at our best. If we have no anxiety, then we are not motivated to give our best effort. I illustrate this for my Introduction to Psychology students by demonstrating what an instructor who had no anxiety would look like showing up for the first class. I quite casually address the students and indicate to them that I have no plan and don't really care what we do for the semester. I indicate that we can spend the semester hanging out or doing whatever we want. This usually brings out more than a few laughs from the students, and they understand the point that I am making.

I go on to demonstrate what the opposite side of the continuum looks like when someone has too much anxiety. I once again address them as if it were the first day of class, but I fidget anxiously with my papers and stumble over my words. Many students quickly become quite uncomfortable and feel sorry for an instructor who is this nervous. I, too, can only demonstrate this behavior for so long until I get uncomfortable with it. However, my point is made.

Too little or too much anxiety can be problematic. There is a psychological principle known as the Yerkes-Dodson law.[26] This principle states that our performance is best when our physiological arousal or anxiety is at moderate levels. The question for you individually is, when it comes to a particular situation or skills, *what is the "right" amount of anxiety for you to be motivated to perform at your best?* That is something that is critical for you to determine in different environments and situations. It is also going to be a critical component to determine how much anxiety is going to help you respond most effectively to situations that involve incivility.

Now that we have established that anxiety has a purpose in our lives and can be a useful source of motivation, you need to understand how to modulate your anxiety most effectively. Breathing is one of the most important but least used skills that can help us regulate ourselves physiologically and, therefore, emotionally. Let's explore breathing more specifically.

Breathing As A Skill

People use different terms to describe skills associated with breathing. Sometimes, it is called abdominal breathing. Other people call it yoga breathing, diaphragmatic breathing, belly breathing, or simply deep breathing. There are also many different approaches to breathing, so I am going to be offering you my take on the ways to use breathing most effectively.

When it comes to using breathing for self-regulation, I have had more than a few clients roll their eyes when I begin to discuss the idea of helping them learn to breathe differently. I often hear, "I already know how to do that, but it does not work for me. Let's go on to something else that would be useful."

I think there are many reasons why people struggle with the use of breathing. One of the major ones is that it takes time to practice, and we have become a "drive-through" society. We want to solve our problems with the quickest solutions. "Is there a pill for that? What is the fastest route from A to B?" We can all fall into this trap, me included. It is important to recognize that when it comes to breathing, this is a skill that will take time for you to develop. Although no skill works for everyone all the time, I would encourage you not to give up easily, because breathing has a great power to help no matter what is happening.

When we first come into the world as babies, we are excellent at the skill of deep breathing. If you have the chance to watch a baby breathing, especially when they are sleeping, you will see that their stomachs are going up and down. We are natural belly breathers and good at deep relaxation at this age. Somewhere along the way, we begin to internalize the stress of the world, and our breathing morphs into a different style. The focus of our breaths becomes much higher in our bodies, up in our chests. We take short, fast, shallow breaths on a regular basis if we are not fully aware of them.

Shallow breathing contributes to greater levels of anxiety and stress since we are not getting the full capacity of oxygen into our lungs. That is why it is important for you to not flip the page to the next chapter, because "this is boring stuff. What else do you got, John?"

I have more on breathing—because I want to encourage you to spend time learning and practicing what may be the most powerful skill you learn in this book.

The Mechanics Of Breathing

When I start coaching someone in the skill of deep breathing, I always demonstrate to them how we breathe most regularly when we are not thinking about it. I take a deep breath, but my shoulders rise, as does my chest as I take a quick breath. I tell people that this is how I, too, can take a deep breath if I am not concentrating.

I then put my hand on my stomach and demonstrate the skill of deep breathing. As I show my client how to take a much slower and deeper breath, the hand on my stomach moves outward as I breathe in and then moves back toward my spine as I breathe out. When we are breathing deeply, we are filling our lungs to a much fuller capacity and therefore pushing our stomach outward.

In this demonstration, I also illustrate how someone can be focused on trying to breathe abdominally but still move their shoulders upward and have the breath still rooted in their chest. This type of breathing can still trigger greater levels of stress and anxiety. I often find myself getting dizzy after just a few of those breaths in a demonstration to a client.

If you are curious about this skill and want to develop it further, I would suggest that you take some time on your own away from others so that you will not feel self-conscious. I encourage you to lie down, stand up, or sit in a chair that allows you to have your body at a 90-degree angle so that your legs are not pushing against your stomach. You want your body posture to allow for an expansion of the lower part of your lungs, which will push your belly outward.

If you can lie down when you first start practicing this type of breathing, I encourage you to do so. Put a pillow on your stomach—many people find it helpful to have a visual of a pillow that they move up and down with their breath. This will also help you to recognize when you are still breathing in your chest. If you're standing up or seated, I would encourage you to put a hand on your chest and a hand on your stomach. This will allow you to monitor for movement in either place. Ideally, you want very little movement in your chest and the predominant movement to occur in your belly.

> Ideally, you want very little movement in your chest and the predominant movement to occur in your belly.

Deep breathing is not a skill to be rushed. Breathe gently through your nose and exhale slowly through your mouth. Pause after you have taken a breath in, and pause after you have exhaled. This will help you to be very focused on each component of the movement and notice how your body feels as you take slower and deeper breaths.

When I practice this with clients for the first time, I demonstrate the skill and then coach them to be sure that they are, in fact, using it correctly. I then invite them to take two minutes to practice abdominal breathing. I promise them that I am not going to simply sit there and observe their breathing but rather focus on my own abdominal breathing and let them experience the difference on their own.

I set the timer on my smartphone for two minutes, and we then sit in silence and breathe. I tell them in advance what my questions are going to be at the end of this time. After we finish, I then follow up with these two questions:

- How well do you think that you were able to do this skill?
- What did you notice (if anything) as you did this skill or now that you have finished?

Many people will report that they feel "a little calmer" or that they feel "more centered." Some people will report feeling sleepy, and others may say that they began to experience warmth or a sensation of "letting go" spreading through their body. I share with people that after a minute or two of deep breathing, I notice a heaviness in my eyes and that my body is sinking into the chair. It always feels like such a relief, and I often reflect in that moment that I should be doing this skill more myself.

Sometimes, people report becoming very dizzy. If this happens to you, you are likely not breathing abdominally but rather continuing to do chest breathing. You may also be breathing too fast and need to slow down your pace.

I have also learned through my clinical experiences that there is another reason that deep breathing is sometimes difficult for people or maybe a skill that they cannot use. One of my specialties as a psychotherapist has been to work with trauma survivors. There is a subgroup of people who have experienced trauma who become highly anxious when focusing inward or on their body. For these people, they will develop a higher level of anxiety when trying to use this skill. We usually identify this very quickly, and I direct them toward other strategies that are likely more effective.

Please keep this in mind if you are someone who has this reaction to deep breathing. I would encourage you not to give up too quickly just because you have experienced trauma. Many trauma survivors can use the skill of abdominal breathing with great success. However, please also remember that no skill works for everybody and that this is not something that you are doing wrong if it can't work for you. I would encourage you to instead check out the skill of grounding that I will describe elsewhere in this book.

Different Approaches To Breathing

As I mentioned earlier, there are many different approaches to breathing—too many to review comprehensively in this text. Below, you will find the breathing strategies that I use the most and encourage clients to use. Once you have mastered the basic mechanics of breathing, you can try applying them in various ways.

Four-Square Breathing

This breathing strategy encourages you to use counting to bring a steady, slow rhythm to your breathing. Four-square breathing uses the number four to regulate breath. You start by taking a deep, slow breath in to the count of four, then hold your breath to the count of four, exhale to the count of four, and pause to the count of four.

In practice, this sounds like, "Breathe in, two, three, four; hold, two, three, four; exhale, two, three, four; hold, two, three, four." Saying this mantra over and over gives the mind something to do and helps people to stay focused on the process of breathing.

Breathing Mantra

Like the four-square breathing method, breathing with a mantra gives our mind something to do. As you may know, a mantra is a phrase or a word that is repeated to help people to better focus and concentrate. In this case, your mantra can be a word or phrase that is particularly meaningful to you. I give my clients examples such as "I breathe in peace, and I exhale stress." "I relax [breathing in] and let go [breathing out]." If you are going to try this, I would suggest that you take some time to think about what words or phrases feel most comfortable for you.

Breathing With Imagery

Some people respond well to auditory stimulation whereas others are more comfortable with visual stimulation. For those of you out there who are more comfortable with images, breathing with imagery is more likely to be your jam.

This type of deep breathing is just as it sounds. I encourage my clients who want to use this skill to imagine a place where they experience a deep sense of relaxation. I live on the coast of Maine, where we can easily access many beautiful beaches and rocky coast formations where we can sit and enjoy the beauty of the ocean. I encourage people to think about a place like this that allows them to feel a deep sense of relaxation. It may be a real place that they have been or would like to visit, or it may be an imaginary place that does not exist. The only requirement is that it's where you can stay completely relaxed. Avoid any place associated with a painful or negative experience—the target is complete relaxation.

Once you have chosen an image that works for you, find a comfortable place to sit and get into a comfortable position lying down or seated with your body at a 90-degree angle. You could close your eyes or leave them open—if you leave them open, focus on a spot across the room where you can fix your gaze. Bring up your relaxation image, then focus on your breathing. As you continue to breathe, you may notice that the image shifts and changes with a greater level of detail, or it may stay static. There is no right way to do this—just be aware of what you observe.

Breathing With Music
Over the years, I've worked with many people who have learned to use music with breathing for stress management and relaxation. Some people want to use heavy metal or acid rock for relaxation. I am not going to be dismissive of this music if you believe it works for you. (In fact, I had a student in my Introduction to Psychology class who informed me that his entire wedding would feature heavy metal pieces that were particularly meaningful to him and his future wife.)

There are others who want to choose pop songs or country music as their source of relaxation. I am not going to argue about your taste in music. I'll just point out that these types of songs have familiar words that we want to sing. When we start to sing, even in our minds, we become more focused on the song and lose focus on the skill we are trying to use.

I often encourage people to choose music that has no lyrics and that is not likely to be a source of distraction or memory association with other times in their lives. I share with people some of my favorite classical pieces of music. I also suggest that they explore new age music that has soothing rhythms. There actually are composers in this genre who create sounds that stimulate our brain in a way that will enhance relaxation. Find what works for you.

Once you have determined the music that is most effective for you, find a quiet place where you can focus. Once again, either lie down or sit in an upright position with your body at a 90-degree angle. Turn on your preferred piece of music and either close your eyes or fix your gaze on a spot across the room.

Listen to the sounds of the music while also focusing on the mechanics of deep breathing. Keep listening to the same piece of music repeatedly. Over time, something very cool can happen. If you get your body relaxed while associating it with this piece of music, you will be able to use this to your benefit in the future.

Once you have paired deep relaxation with this piece of music, your body will automatically begin to relax when it hears the familiar tune. This effect is based on a psychological principle known as "classical conditioning." Things that continue to occur together are things that we then expect to experience together. Once your body hears that piece of music, it will expect relaxation and, therefore, go into autopilot to make that happen.

Different Applications Of The Skill

You have been very patient in listening to my descriptions of the mechanics and benefits of deep breathing. However, you might be sitting there thinking, "How is this going to benefit me?" I am so glad that you asked because it means that you are interested in learning more. There are two ways in which I advise clients to use breathing in the long term and short term. Let's start by looking at the long term.

Long-Term Applications

Deep relaxation comes from regular practice of a skill. If breathing is going to work for you, then you will need to set aside time to practice it on a regular basis, ideally daily. Set aside five to ten minutes to practice it a few times a day if you can. Don't get caught up thinking that you must practice a minimum number of times or that it is simply a waste. Any amount of time that you can practice breathing will be beneficial for you and your stress level.

Just like any skill, deep breathing is something that gets better with practice. It is therefore important to continue to work to perfect this skill and to practice keeping your chest mostly still and creating more movement in your lower abdomen. This gets easier over time, to the point where you can more quickly get into the posture and rhythm of effective deep breathing.

Abdominal breathing will be most helpful when you are managing the overall effects of uncivil behavior on the part of others. You can use this type of breathing before you enter a stressful environment, which is the source of difficulty. For example, you can take five or ten minutes at home in the morning as part of your routine before you leave for work. I've also advised clients to pull up to work but pause before they get out of their car. I tell them to spend five or ten minutes doing deep breathing right there in the parking lot before they go into the building. In this way, they are inoculating themselves against the potential stress of the day.

You can then sprinkle episodes of deep breathing for a few minutes throughout your day. If you are doing this subtly, you can do it at your desk while remaining seated. Some people cannot find any private place in their office except for the bathroom. If that is your only refuge, then you should use it. You may want to take a few extra minutes for every bathroom trip that you take to focus on breathing.

You can then have another, perhaps longer, episode of deep breathing as you transition home to let go and release the stresses that have built up over the course of your day. Remember that breathing has a great deal of power to shift your physiology.

Are you in an environment that has significant stress and incivility? Remember that you do not exist in those types of environments unscathed and that you will likely carry the effects of being in that situation with you throughout other parts of your life. Breathing can be the key to releasing at least some of those burdens.

Short-Term Applications

"Hang on just a minute—I need to do my deep breathing for ten minutes, and then I'll get back to you."

Life doesn't work like this. In a stressful situation, we don't always have time to focus on breathing. But the more you practice it in situations that aren't stressful, the easier it'll be when stress pops up unexpectedly. Even when you are in a heated discussion with colleagues, you can try deep breathing slowly and without taking audible exhales, and you will be able to do this quite subtly.

As you start to notice sources of frustration or irritation, you can bring your attention to taking a few slow, deep breaths. If someone is being uncivil or saying things to anger you, you can gently distract yourself from their behavior and quickly bring your focus to your breath for just a few seconds. We will talk more about this when I describe the four-step mindfulness. However, in the short term, I am suggesting that you use your breath as a momentary source of grounding to help you calm your body and, therefore, be more likely to respond as opposed to react.

Conclusion

Breathing is a foundational but often overlooked skill when it comes to regulating our bodies and our emotions. As I encourage everyone: don't *underestimate* the potential impact breathing can have on your ability to be skillful in the face of incivility or *overestimate* your ability to use it by thinking that it is a "really easy skill" (it isn't—it takes practice) or that you don't really need to practice it (you do). Breathing serves as a core component of the upcoming skills in this section of the book, so before you turn the page, be sure that you have given yourself enough time to develop this skill.

> As I encourage everyone: don't *underestimate* the potential impact breathing can have on your ability to be skillful in the face of incivility . . .

The Least You Need To Know

- Breathing is a foundational skill for managing anxiety and reactivity to others or situations that involve incivility.

- A certain amount of anxiety is beneficial in our lives to help us function at our best.

- As adults, we often lose awareness of our breath and breathe quite shallowly, which makes stressful situations and our reactions to them worse.

- Learning the proper approach to breathing takes time and effort, but it is worth it.

- Once we develop our ability to do deep breathing, we can use it as a strategy for stress management both in the short and long term.

chapter five

Acceptance:
How To Live With Our Emotions

As I am sitting here typing out the start of this chapter, the rain is pouring down in buckets. When it gets particularly rainy like this, and you go out into the world and talk to people in stores or restaurants, you'll often hear complaints about the rain.

"I can't stand another rainy day," said one woman to me recently. "This is not fair."

A couple in line at the grocery store said to one another, "We should be getting more sun. Summer is what we wait for in Maine, and this rain is ruining things completely."

While I have feedback I could provide to these and other members of the public, I don't challenge someone's cognitive distortions while waiting to check out at the grocery store. However, when I am in my office, and I hear a client speaking in this way, I know that this is an opportunity to think about a concept that can be of help to them. I know it's helpful because it has been of help to me—the concept of "acceptance." And acceptance just so happens to be a critical skill to use when faced with an experience of incivility. How so? Read on.

What Is Acceptance?

Acceptance from a Buddhist standpoint is about "acknowledging what is." You may not like or agree with what is happening, but you are simply noting reality and dealing with facts. Let's explore this a little further and see what some other authors have to say about this.

> You may not like or agree with what is happening,
> but you are simply noting reality and dealing with facts.

Views From Other Experts

In *The Mindfulness Solution,* Dr. Ronald Siegel writes that trying to develop an attitude of acceptance is perhaps the most important but most difficult part of trying to approach life mindfully. However, he notes that, "acceptance allows us to be open to both pleasure and pain, to embrace both winning and losing, and to be compassionate with ourselves and others when mistakes are made. Acceptance allows us to say yes to the parts of a personality we want to eliminate or hide."[27]

In their book *Mindfulness: An Eight-Week Plan to Finding Peace in a Frantic World,* Drs. Mark Williams and Danny Penman describe how the root of the word acceptance means "to receive or to take hold of something." They reported how clients can think that acceptance means "passive resignation" or "giving up," and I would echo this idea. Clients often recoil at the notion of acceptance as "giving in or letting others win." These authors noted instead that acceptance is "a pause, a period of allowing, of letting be, of clear seeing. Acceptance takes us off the hair trigger so that we are less likely to make a knee-jerk reaction. It allows us to become fully aware of difficulties, with all their painful nuances, and respond to them in the most skillful way possible."[28]

Other authors have put it more simply. "Acceptance refers to a willingness to let things be just as they are the moment we become aware of them—accepting pleasurable and painful experiences as they are."[29] These authors noted that acceptance, in this sense, adds "friendliness or kindness" to our approach to difficulties in life.

My View

When I talk to my clients about the concept of acceptance, I usually start with this latter definition of acknowledging the facts of reality in the moment. I encourage people to step back and identify the parts of reality that they don't like or agree with and try to examine how they are "fighting reality." My previous example of weather is one that many of you can likely relate to, and perhaps you can think of other ways you have fought reality yourself.

I also remember a client who had moved from Maine to San Francisco and then moved back. He would often bemoan the weather in Maine and talk about how much better the weather was in San Francisco, even though it was not affordable for him to live there. When he started to talk like this, I would do my most brilliant clinical intervention by leaning forward in my chair and saying the following: "You are not in San Francisco. You are in Maine. Until you are in San Francisco, you are in Maine." After a while, he would burst out laughing as I would repeat this same phrase to him (like a recording), and he would catch himself in a mode of nonacceptance.

I always joke that people move to Maine in July when it is sunny, beautiful weather, and they will talk about how excited they are to be here. I smile and nod while inside, I am thinking, "Wait until January." Many of these same people will run screaming for the border when we have our third or fourth day in a row of subzero temperatures. I always say, "January thins the herd in Maine."

Pain Versus Suffering

In the language of Buddhism, there is an important distinction between pain and suffering. We tend to use these words often interchangeably in standard English, but they are different concepts and important to separate, especially when it comes to accepting reality.

Pain is a part of life. I wish that last sentence were not true, but unfortunately, it is. The experience of living will include physical and emotional pain. We cannot get around this reality and, therefore, need to accept it.

Pain also has a purpose. When I begin to talk about this, I often get quizzical looks from my clients until I explain further what I mean. Physical pain tells us that something is wrong in the body. It gets our attention and causes us to stop to figure out what may be out of balance. Pain also tells us that we need to find a solution to the physical imbalance that we are experiencing, which may involve consulting our doctor or, in extreme cases, going to the emergency room.

Emotional pain also has a purpose. When we feel distress or sadness, we may be experiencing the loss of someone or something that was important to us. In the beginning of humankind, this pain of loss when someone was missing from the group caused others to go looking for that individual. That same thing could be true even today if we have not heard from someone for a while and we are concerned about them. The emotional pain we experience in anger can signal to us that we are experiencing an injustice or feel as if our rights have been violated. Emotional pain tells us that something out of balance needs our attention.

> Emotional pain tells us that something out of balance needs our attention.

Suffering, in a Buddhist sense, does not have to be a part of life, although it often is for many of us. "Suffering" is fighting reality or "not accepting what is." In everyday language, we can say that someone is suffering from a cold or suffering with chronic pain. However, in the Buddhist sense, suffering is about a lack of acceptance of reality. My client, who is chronically complaining about the weather in Maine, was engaging in suffering. It is true that the weather in New England can sometimes cause our plans to be changed or make things difficult for us (pain), but it does not, in fact, have to "ruin" our day or our week (suffering).

Curiosity

Before the COVID-19 pandemic, I enjoyed traveling to visit friends, and I am now slowly getting back into my globetrotting ways. I often travel to meetings with other psychologists and coaches as I remain active in many professional organizations. Although more meetings are happening virtually these days, I find that in-person meetings are the most effective way for me to network with and learn from others.

One trip included four flights with brief stays at various locations in between. On that trip, my luggage was temporarily lost on three of the four flights. Yes, you read that correctly. It was lost on *three of the four flights*. That is often my fate when I travel. I have had to show up at professional meetings wearing shorts and a T-shirt because my baggage was delayed—much to the enjoyment of my colleagues, I'm sure.

I used to get anxious and even annoyed when I went to stand at the baggage carousel and wait for my luggage. I could feel myself tensing up and holding myself hostage until my eyes spotted my bag, and I could then relax. After learning and teaching people mindfulness (and learning to practice it more on my own), I realized that I needed to use mindfulness skills in this situation.

I recognized that I needed to use *curiosity* to help me with my luggage drama. Understanding that I could do little to change the fate of what happens with my baggage, as I approach the luggage carousel, I tell myself, "Let's see what happens. Let's see if my luggage shows up." Dan Harris describes this skill as "non-attachment to results."[30]

If the luggage appears, it is a nice surprise. If it does not, I know what to do (having done it many times). For example, I was recently at an airport waiting for my bag and suddenly saw someone take what looked like my luggage off the carousel. I thought, "That cannot be my luggage." Fast forward to the end of the luggage carousel, and my bag was not there. I was then called by airline staff to report to the baggage office. I thought for sure that my luggage was in Tuscaloosa. However, it turned out that airline staff had mistaken my bag for one that was left over from a previous flight and moved it to their office. I was able to have a happy reunion with my bag. If I had been stuck in panic mode about my belongings, I would have created unnecessary stress.

You may be now thinking, "John, what does luggage retrieval have to do with incivility?" Read on. Trust that I will be "bringing this all home" before the chapter is done. I want to make sure that you first understand the concept. Stay tuned.

How Do You Practice Acceptance?

One strategy to practice acceptance is something I noted above: *curiosity*. If you practice an attitude of curiosity, you will find that it helps you to "step back" from being too attached to a specific outcome of a situation. Naturally, we all want things to go "our way" or a certain way that we think is "best." However, we cannot guarantee that, and approaching situations—especially difficult or distressing situations—with curiosity is one important skill we can use to practice acceptance.

Acceptance: How To Live With Our Emotions | 75

> If you practice an attitude of curiosity, you will find that it helps you to "step back" from being too attached to a specific outcome of a situation.

When it comes to managing pain or distress, we must first consider the root causes of lack of acceptance. At times, we can get caught up in the nonacceptance of reality with our minds. At other times, the source of fighting reality has to do with our bodies—like in the story of waiting for my bags, before I even arrived at the carousel, I could feel myself tensing up as soon as I got off the plane. The tension we hold in our bodies can sometimes feed our nonacceptance of reality.

Below you will see a few strategies that you can use to help promote acceptance of things as they are. Keep in mind that acceptance of reality does not mean a lack of hope of change. Rather, acceptance is a first step to then more mindfully plan how we will change the situation or our approach to it.

Acceptance With The Body

Dialectical Behavior Therapy (DBT) is the first place that I learned more formally about the skill of acceptance. DBT includes a set of skills based around what it calls "radical acceptance."[31] I think that DBT describes acceptance as "radical" in this situation because those seeking to use DBT skills are "suffering" (in the sense we have described above) with *deep* distress.[32]

Radical acceptance is needed to push away the intense distress that we can feel. Therefore, the solution is to find ways to release the tension in our bodies. There are many DBT distress tolerance skills we can learn, but here are a few strategies to accept reality with the body:

- *Breathing*. You have already learned about different approaches to deep breathing and how helpful they can be in allowing you to feel calmer and more present in a situation. Breathing allows us to release body tension and is one strategy to accept reality with the body.

- *Half-smiling.* The *facial feedback hypothesis* posits that our facial expressions impact our emotional state. DBT describes the skill of "half-smiling." This expression is not a smirk or a fake smile. It is a smile in which your facial muscles are relaxed, and your expression is somewhat neutral, but the corners of your mouth are slightly turned upward. It is also known as an "enigmatic smile," an expression made famous by Leonardo da Vinci's painting *Mona Lisa*. I often try to use half-smiling when I am caught in traffic. Remember that accepting reality does not mean that it becomes neutral or good. Accepting reality means that it is not more intensely distressing and becomes manageable.

- *Willing hands.* The *behavioral feedback hypothesis* states that our body posture communicates our emotional state to our brain in a circular loop. Clenching our fists is an example of fighting reality. "Willing hands" can be done whether we are standing, sitting, or lying down. In any of these positions, our hands are open, fingers are relaxed, and our palms are turned outward or upward. The specifics of each position are as follows:

  - *Standing.* Allow your arms to hang down from your shoulders in a relaxed state. Keep your hands open, with your palms open and thumbs to the side.

  - *Sitting*: Rest your hands on your lap or on your thighs. Palms are turned upward, and thumbs relax gently to each side.

  - *Lying down*: Arms are by your side, and hands face upward with palms open.

> Accepting reality means that it is not more
> intensely distressing and becomes manageable.

Acceptance With The Mind

Dr. Steven Hayes is a well-known psychologist who created a form of treatment known as Acceptance and Commitment Therapy (ACT).[33] Mindfulness serves as the foundation of this model of therapy, which posits that our lack of acceptance of our inner experience is the cause of much of our distress. ACT says that we end up avoiding new behaviors that could be good for us because of how overwhelmed we are by internal distress. (If you are curious to learn more, I would encourage you to read *ACT Made Simple* by Dr. Russ Harris.)[34][35]

Sometimes, our source of tension has to do with negative thinking about ourselves or situations that leave us fighting reality. I will hear people say things like "It is not fair" or "I can't stand this." We will be talking about skills of mindfulness that can help shift our minds away from the source of distress. I will give you a few ideas here and expand on them in the chapters of mindfulness. Here are some things to try:

- *Cognitive diffusion.* This strategy comes directly from ACT. In short, ACT encourages you to disentangle yourself from your thoughts. You are not your thoughts but rather are having thoughts. You can notice, "Oh, wow. I'm having really irritated thoughts right now about being in this meeting when I really need to be working." "Huh, I'm noticing how I'm thinking that this person on the highway in front of me should move over." Work to control your mind so that your mind does not control you. We will review this in greater detail later in the book.

- *Turning the mind.* This strategy from DBT is about recognizing that you are fighting reality and visualizing yourself at a crossroads. In one direction, you can see yourself traveling toward acceptance. In the other direction, you can see the reality that you want but that does not exist in this moment. You can also think of this as the "reality-accepting" road in one direction and the "reality-fighting" road in the other direction. Tell yourself that you are going to choose the reality-accepting road. When your mind wants to do a detour back, remind it that you are no longer choosing that road.

Sometimes my GPS wants to send me in directions that I don't want to go or that don't make sense. In a similar way, your brain could be wanting to take you in directions that you don't want. Gently ignore it and stay on the road of acceptance.

- *Willingness.* This strategy, also from DBT, is about challenging your thinking and adopting a more flexible approach to a situation. Your goal is to examine if you are fighting reality. Willingness replaces willfulness when we are attempting to "fix" or "control" every situation. DBT describes willfulness as "an attachment to *me, me, me*, and what I want *right now.*" Willingness is acting with awareness and doing what is effective in a situation.

The Guest House

I share this reflection with many clients who are struggling to overcome symptoms or who are struggling with a life event that has just occurred, and their lack of acceptance is causing them distress.

"The Guest House" by Rūmī is a poem that illustrates the idea of acceptance. Rūmī was a thirteenth-century Persian Sufi mystic, poet, and theologian. He was known for writing both poems and texts that preached love and acceptance of others. Although his work is based on the tenets of Islam, his teachings have a universality of application and can be referenced in a variety of religious and cultural environments.

I would invite you to take a few minutes to sit somewhere and read this poem *mindfully*. Yes, mindfully. I would invite you to stop doing the twelve other things that you are doing now. Find a comfortable place to sit, take a few deep breaths, and read this poem slowly to yourself (or maybe to your dog or cat), but listen with your head and your heart. What do I mean by that? I am suggesting that you listen to both your cognitive and emotional reactions.

The Guest House[36]
Jalāl ad-Dīn Muhammad Rūmī
Translated by Coleman Barks

This being human is a guest house.
Every morning a new arrival.
A joy, a depression, a meanness,
some momentary awareness comes
as an unexpected visitor.
Welcome and entertain them all!
Even if they're a crowd of sorrows,
who violently sweep your house
empty of its furniture,
still, treat each guest honorably.
He may be clearing you out
for some new delight.
The dark thought, the shame, the malice,
meet them at the door laughing,
and invite them in.
Be grateful for whoever comes,
because each has been sent
as a guide from beyond.

(Pause here if you would like to reflect on your reactions.)

So, what did you notice? What reactions did you have? What parts did you like? What parts were difficult for you? Consider taking a few minutes to write down your reactions.

The purpose of "The Guest House" is to indicate how our experiences in life are transient. Just like the quip attributed to Mark Twain about the weather in New England—"If you don't like it, wait a minute"—our associations and reactions will change "if we just wait a minute." (Okay, it may take more than a minute, but the point is that how we experience things can change). If we hang on to our experiences and refuse to move on from them, then we are "suffering," and our pain intensifies or stays around longer. I always tell clients to "leave the doors and windows of their guest house open so that experiences can come and go."

How Can Acceptance Help With Incivility?

So, how can acceptance help with incivility? Sometimes, the source of incivility is our own thinking and the ways that we fight reality. At other times, we are dealing with the behavior of others.

Internal

I was born and raised in Massachusetts, where, as I like to say, "driving is a contact sport." When you drive in Massachusetts (especially around Boston), you must drive assertively on the roads, or you may be run over. Even though I moved to Maine many years ago, I still carry those Massachusetts driving habits somewhere deep in my DNA. I know when I get behind the wheel of a car that I must be prepared for others who may have a less assertive—or one might say "planful"—approach to driving.

When I drive, I remind myself that I am not a driving instructor for the world. Others may be drifting into my lane or slowing down for no apparent reason. My coaching them on what they need to do differently is not going to change their habits. My task is to accept what they are doing as reality (not fighting what they should/should not be doing) and then determine how I can best respond.

Think of that person in front of you as you are walking into a building, who opens the door and then lets it slam in your face behind them. You may find yourself wanting to scream, *"Hello? I am a human here behind you."* You may find yourself feeling offended or irritated. *"What is wrong with them?"* Instead of letting those thoughts fester into irritation, you then carry them with you, notice that you have them, and accept them. You can then decide what you want to do. Often, saying nothing may be your best option.

External

Imagine that you are in a meeting, and your boss is expressing thanks to members of a team who worked on a major project that was successfully completed. She mentions everyone on the team *except you*. No one else speaks up, and then the meeting goes on. You are sitting there finding your thoughts spinning on the fact that you were left out and how unfair this is. If you sit in the rest of the meeting and focus on being left out, your level of irritation may remain high or even grow. The bigger that it grows, the more likely you are to react at some point about this.

Use acceptance to gain perspective and decide what to do. Typically, it's best to pause and wait to respond when you are calmer and have the chance to think through how to handle the situation. You might even consult others to decide on a course of action. Skills later in the book will help you do so skillfully if you decide to speak up.

Conclusion

Acceptance is an important skill when we are dealing with the stresses of life. As you have learned, acceptance is not about giving up or giving in, but rather, it is a choice that we make to work toward seeing reality as it is (not as we want it to be).

Acceptance skills can help us to "step back" and observe what is happening in the moment, which allows us to be less emotionally engaged. This will tie in with other mindfulness strategies we will review later in the book. However, you will need to accept that we are not there yet but going on now to talk about four-step mindfulness.

The Least You Need To Know

- Acceptance is a skill in which we acknowledge reality as it is, not as we wish it to be.

- Pain (physical and emotional) is a part of life, but suffering (in a Buddhist sense, nonacceptance of pain) does not have to be.

- Approaching life with curiosity, especially situations that we anticipate may be difficult, can help us be less reactive and more skillful.

- There are many strategies that we can use to accept reality with our body and our mind.

- Acceptance skills can be of use, whether the source of incivility is internal or external.

chapter six

Four-Step Mindfulness: How To Handle Our Reactions

I was a graduate student (or, as a colleague in our program called it, "gradual student") at Michigan State, so this was, ahem, more than a few years ago. However, I remember this situation as if it were yesterday.

As a student, I had the opportunity to serve as a faculty assistant. I was fortunate enough to work for my academic advisor, Linda Forrest. Linda and I ran eight-session seminars for teachers looking for new careers and offered them vocational counseling to consider these options. Part of this seminar involved individualized testing for areas of skills and strengths using well-researched measures.

A week after dropping off the completed surveys that needed to be computer-scored, I returned to the testing office to get the results. At that time, computers were much larger and needed more time to process information. Unfortunately, I was told that there was a backlog of work and that they did not have the results yet, but to come back the following week. I smiled and agreed to do so. When I returned a week later, I was told there had been additional delays and that the survey results were still not ready. I was to return in five more days to get the results.

When I came to the office for the third time to get the results, the technician informed me that the results were *still not ready*. Feeling a rising frustration, I began to take a deep breath to simply calm myself. Before I said anything, the technician immediately said, "Don't get angry at me! This is not my fault. I won't have it."

I informed her that I was simply taking a deep breath to then figure out the next step. However, I will admit that I was frustrated and that, in fact, I could feel anger building at being accused of something that I was not feeling.

Fortunately, I kept my "wits about me" and agreed to return the fourth time. When I did, the results were ready, and all was well with the staff. Little did I know at the time that I was applying a skill that I would formally understand years later: four-step mindfulness.

My Learning Of Mindfulness

I first was exposed to skills of mindfulness when I was trained in 1998 in DBT. DBT skills are helpful for clients who have experienced trauma and who are experiencing significant reactivity in their lives.[37] The skills focus on learning to tolerate distress, being more effective interpersonally, managing emotions, and using mindfulness to be aware of the present moment. Mindfulness serves as the core of the skills and became an area of interest and personal practice for me after I first attended this training.

Wanting to learn more about mindfulness and not wanting to go to a Buddhist monastery to meditate for days or hours, I sought out further training. I enrolled in a seminar on mindfulness for therapists taught by Terry Fralich. Terry has extensive training in meditation founded on a richness of experience studying with great teachers, including the Dalai Lama himself.

Terry's training taught me many practical mindfulness skills that I use personally and share with clients. These skills include the four-step mindfulness. An expanded explanation of this skill can be found in Terry's book, *Cultivating Lasting Happiness*, which I highly recommend.[38]

In addition, I am a huge fan of the books on mindfulness written by Dan Harris. *10% Happier* and *Meditation for Fidgety Skeptics* are a central part of the foundational strategies that I teach clients as they are very practical and "on-the-go" mindfulness skills.[39] I encourage you to review these as well as you grow your own mindfulness practice.

Finally, I would highlight the writings and work of Jon Kabat-Zinn. His books *Full Catastrophe Living* and *Wherever You Go, There You Are* played a central role in the development of my mindfulness practice, along with attending several of his trainings.[40]

Four-Step Mindfulness Explained

This skill is useful to help us respond effectively in situations instead of reacting. As you may remember, *reacting* is something we do that is emotion-based and involves little to no thinking, while *responding* is the more skillful way that we determine "the best way forward" or "what is most effective" in a situation. Rather than getting caught up in what is "right or fair," we can focus instead on what is most useful or practical to do in a specific situation.

Four-step mindfulness is one of those tools that can help us refocus and respond when emotions begin to disrupt our thought process in a way that can derail us emotionally and cause us unnecessary distress.

It's quite easy to remember:

1. Stop
2. Breathe
3. Reflect
4. Choose

Let's explore each of these steps in greater depth.

Stop

The first thing that you need to do is to stop. In this step, you bring your awareness to the emotional experience that you are having. We are using the mindfulness skills to help us manage our reactivity. Therefore, we are not concerned about emotions that we perceive as positive, such as joy or contentment. Although it is possible to have too many positive feelings and, therefore, make problematic choices, these are very rare events and will not be the primary source of uncivil behaviors. With this skill, we focus more on emotions that will cause us distress or problems. It is these emotions that are likely to hijack our experiences and cause us to act or behave in ways that are not effective.

When Emotions Hijack You

We may have certain emotions that are problematic for us. Many people with whom I work come to treatment presenting with problems in managing anger. Whether the anger is directed at others or against themselves, anger remains the root cause of many destructive behaviors and conflicts.

As you continue to read the steps, think about which emotion or emotions are most problematic for you. Is it frustration? Is it anger, like for many of my clients? Do you find yourself often irritated or impatient? Is the major problem for you that you get very anxious very quickly?

Think about your experience and see if you can begin to recognize what emotion or emotions have the potential to be disruptive in your life. How do you know that you are starting to experience the disruptive feeling that can cause problems? This is a process that I often review with clients. I will ask them, "When did you first start noticing you were feeling irritated?" I will often hear people say that they first noticed the feeling as they were screaming at their child or the clerk in a local store. In short, they do not notice the feeling until it is present in full force. I then encourage people to take some time to explore this process a little further. I can often see that clients put up with me and don't believe they will get anything from stepping back and noticing. However, they are patient with me and agree to begin the exploration process.

I ask them to begin noticing what changes in their thinking or bodily awareness tell them that they are starting to feel the emotion causing them problems. I pull out a great emotion chart from the emotion regulation materials in DBT.

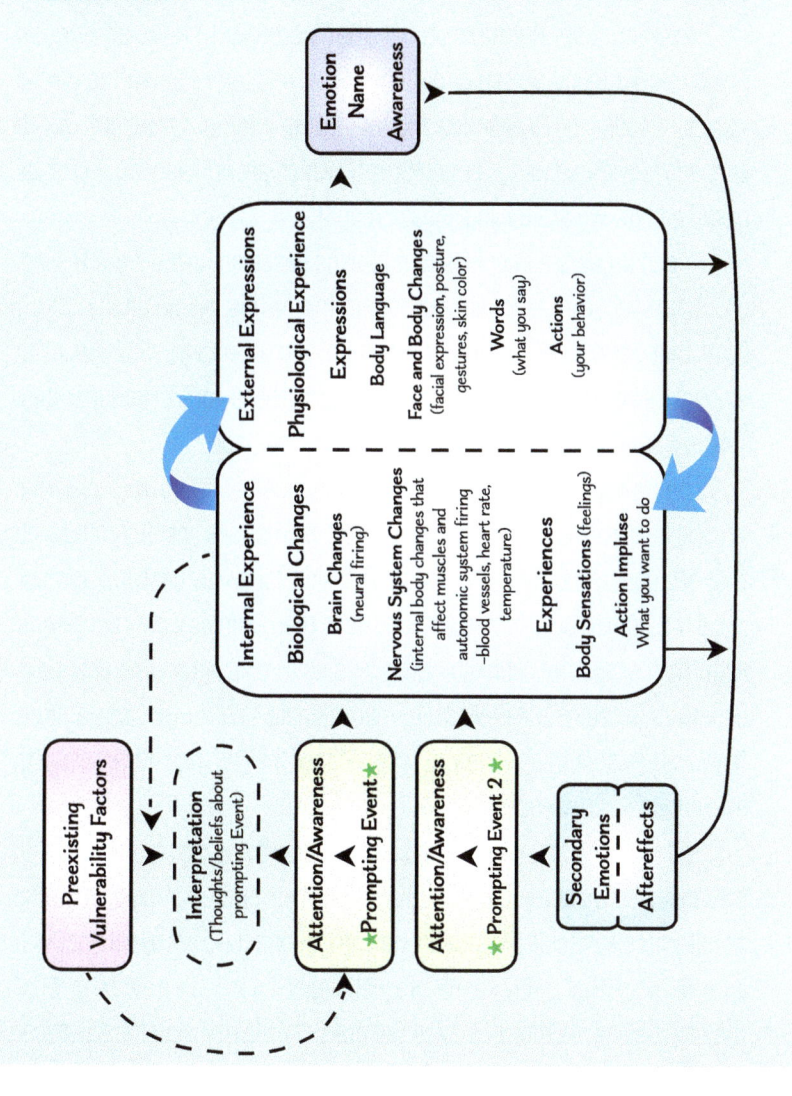

As you can see, the process of an emotional experience begins with a prompting event. Something happens, and that causes us to have an initial start to an emotional response. This event may lead us into a direct physiological experience, or it may take us to an interpretation of the event that leads us into that physiological experience.

As an example, a loud noise may cause us to immediately startle without the need for interpretation, whereas seeing dishes left in the sink at our office could lead to the interpretation that "This is so disrespectful once again."

In either case, the next step is that we begin to have an *internal* response. Our blood pressure, our heart rate, and our temperature can all increase, leading us to experiencing a variety of internal sensations. These sensations will lead us to "action urges," which are impulses to do things based on how we are feeling. Please read that again.

Action urges are impulses to do things based on how we are feeling, which are separate from actually doing them. This will be an important point that we will review later when examining other skills. Still, I want to emphasize here that internal urges and external behavior can be separated. This is what four-step mindfulness will allow you to do.

The next part of the emotional experience has to do with external expressions of emotion. We will have facial expressions and body language that are generated by the emotion. Our skin tone, our posture, and our vocal tone can all be affected and lead us to then express words consistent with the feelings. This can ultimately lead us to take action and engage in behaviors based on the feeling. For many people, action urges and actions feel like the same thing for them, when in fact they are two different parts of emotional experience.

The final step in the initial experience of emotion is our awareness of its presence. You will see in the chart that having had an internal experience and an external expression of emotion, we can label what we are experiencing. It is at this point that many people are just beginning to have a sense of what they are feeling. As the old expression goes, "It is like closing the barn door after the horses have already gotten out." At this point, the person has likely already acted on the feeling and engaged in behaviors that they may regret.

You will see that the last step in this chart involves the aftereffects of an emotion. These aftereffects could be physical, or they also could be other emotions. For example, after someone has gotten extremely angry, the aftereffect may be that their heart continues to race, and they find themselves continuing to clench their fists and scowl. Their initial experience of anger can also trigger additional anger and result in a spiral of anger leading to problematic behaviors that then lead to more anger and more problematic behaviors in an ever-increasing cycle of dysfunction.

There is another psychological principle at work here that is important for you to understand. It is called the "facial feedback hypothesis" or the "behavioral feedback hypothesis." The brief explanation of this concept involves the understanding based on neuroscience that our facial expressions and in fact our very behavior don't just reflect what we are feeling but can also *feed* what we are feeling. In other words, if you are feeling angry and your face and body express it, you will be feeding the anger in a cycle that can lead to greater and greater amounts of it. Four-step mindfulness can help you disrupt the cycles and be more skillful.

Now, you have the same understanding of the emotional experience that I share with my clients. I point out to them that, although they may not believe it, their emotions are a process and that emotions do not usually "just happen" without any warning signs. I encourage them and I am encouraging you to take this chart to heart and begin to bring your awareness more fully to how your emotional experience feels to you. Please remember that, in this case, we are particularly interested in the negative emotions that are likely to disrupt your functioning.

So, we use the first step of *stop* to bring our awareness to our negative emotion as soon as possible. We look for warning signs, physically or cognitively, and they can tell us we are starting to have an emotional reaction. As Terry Fralich indicates, we can use these initial warning signs as a cue to tell us, "I need to pay attention to this *now*."[41]

Breathe

Effective deep breathing is a core skill that will be essential for you to learn and practice. It is a foundation of the four-step mindfulness. We have already discussed the power of breathing and the awareness of breath in a previous chapter. But I do want to remind you of its importance in managing your reactivity regarding an urge to be uncivil toward others or in dealing with instability from someone else.

Remember that there are two applications of deep breathing. We can use abdominal breathing to shift our physiology in more profound ways by practicing it for five to ten minutes several times a day. However, there is another version of deep breathing we can use "in the moment" and take a few deep, slow breaths to help ground ourselves in a circumstance. This short-term approach to breathing is what we use in four-step mindfulness.

Once we have *stopped* and identified the negative emotion, we bring our attention to our breath in the moment. We could take a deep breath and slowly exhale. As we exhale, we try to relax our bodies and relax into whatever we are feeling. The goal is to help us soften our emotional experience while pausing.

People often think I am saying that if they take one or two deep breaths, their feeling will magically disappear. I must correct this mistaken belief. Skills are not magic, and our experience does not shift that quickly. Rather, the realistic goal is that breathing will help to perhaps take the edge off the feeling or stop the feeling from escalating further. However, the feeling is not going to go away. This skill is simply allowing us to be in control of our feeling as opposed to our feeling controlling us.

Reflect

Now that you have taken this opportunity to *stop* yourself as you recognize the start of a problematic emotion and *breathe* to take the edge off, your next step is to figure out how you wish to respond effectively. That is what the *reflect* component of four-step mindfulness allows you to do: take time to think.

If you have identified an emotion that causes you to act in negative ways, you probably know what those negative behaviors have been historically for you. Maybe you have thrown things in anger. Perhaps you have made sarcastic comments to people out of irritation.

Recognize your negative behavior patterns and keep them in mind in that very moment. What are your action urges based on this emotion? What have been those old habits that have caused problems? Is your reaction in the moment being influenced by previous experience or messages that you have received? Are you experiencing a reaction in the situation that is mostly being fed by associations to the past?

You can also ask yourself questions about what is more effective to do. What would be the most skillful response that you could have right now? What are the choices before you to engage in a new behavior? What skills have you learned that you could implement now? The *reflect* step is primarily about remembering the new behaviors you have learned and wish to implement.

Choose

Choose is the last step in four-step mindfulness, but I would argue that it is perhaps the most important. Up to this point, you have taken the opportunity to recognize that you are triggered into a negative emotion that has caused problems for you, you have paused, and you have reflected on what options exist for you to engage in a different or more skillful response. The last step is to make a choice in the moment about what to do next.

This all sounds rather easy at this point, doesn't it? You have been able to step back and determine how you are going to respond most effectively in the situation. So, all you need to do is "do it." If only it were that easy. Indeed, after years and years of teaching people to "be mindful" and "do what is effective," I attended a conference in which all of what I had known until that point was challenged. If I had not had my socks glued on, they would have been knocked off. (No, I don't glue my socks; I am simply noting how profound this moment was.)

It was a conference of psychologists who work in organizations, and I attended a workshop on how neuroscience affects behavior. The presenter outlined how deeply engrained our behavior patterns can be when we try to change. He described a concept that had escaped me until that point: *automaticity*. I am going to share with you what he shared with me. I hope that this will help you be more patient with others and with yourself when it comes to behavior change.

Automaticity is a concept that entails behaviors that you engage in unconsciously or automatically. People sometimes use the word "autoroutines" as a synonym for this idea. In short, these are behavior patterns that are deeply ingrained in our experience and for which there are well-worn pathways in our brains.

You have autoroutines for thousands and thousands of behaviors that you do every day without thinking. We learn to do things like brushing our teeth, showering, and getting dressed that quickly become habits that are part of our day, without actual thought about how to do them. Even more complex behaviors like riding a bike or driving a car can become automatic processes that we do without thinking.

The point is our autoroutines for behavior will "kick in" automatically. Here is an example outlined by Robert Eichinger in his talk on neuroscience.[42]

Imagine that you are wandering the streets of your city or town late at night. The streets are deserted, and no one seems to be around. As you continue walking, you notice that someone is coming toward you on the same side of the street. Your brain goes into an autoroutine.

Your brain takes in visual information about the person and then compares this with all the people whom you know. Is that Charlie or Gladys from work? If so, you can relax. However, what if you don't recognize the person? Your brain goes back out to gather more information. What are the qualities of this person coming toward you? Is this someone who might be a threat? Is this a little old lady who is up early (very early) for her morning walk before church, or is it a member of a local motorcycle gang who is sharpening a knife as he walks toward you?

Your brain takes in this information and determines if a threat exists or not. If no threat exists, you just keep walking toward the person. If a threat does exist, however, your brain goes into an autoroutine to have you move to the other side of the street or turn around and run, depending upon the intensity of the threat. Are you with me so far?

Here is the punch line: the entire process that I have outlined above happens in 200 to 300 milliseconds. Wow, that is fast. However, guess what? *We do not even become aware that there is a person there until 500 milliseconds!* Yes, you read that correctly. Your brain has done all that work and made a behavior choice *before awareness kicks in.*

When I first learned this, my mouth dropped wide open, and my eyes grew wide in amazement. Why? Well, I have always told people (and myself) that mindfulness can help us determine the most effective choices for our behavior *before* we act. I realized in that moment that I had been wrong all those years.

Mindfulness is not going to help us in these situations *before* we act. Rather, mindfulness could help us redirect our behavior that was already underway. The horse is on its way out of the barn. We were not starting at the beginning but somewhere in the middle. This is why behavior change is so difficult and why this allegedly "simple" step of "choice" is nowhere near as simple as it seems.

> Rather, mindfulness could help us redirect our behavior that was already underway.

An Uncivil Example

Let's look at an example of four-step mindfulness when it comes to dealing with uncivil behavior on the part of others. Imagine you are at work and, like me, you come upon a stack of unwashed dishes sitting in the break room sink underneath a sign that says, "You are at work, which means you are an adult. Wash your own dishes!"

Someone apparently missed this memo. You immediately find yourself thinking, "Once again, someone else thinks that I am their staff. *How did they miss the sign?* Am I just going to wash someone else's dishes again while gritting my teeth in frustration?" You feel the tension rising in your body, like someone has turned on a furnace in your chest that is gradually making its way up through your neck into your head. You may even feel your face turning red.

1. Stop

You stop yourself as you realize that you are feeling the warning signs of anger. You don't want to let this frustration build and carry this tension around. You also don't want to be snippy with others at work as you try to identify who the culprit might be who is "trying to ruin your day" by putting dirty dishes in your path.

2. Breathe

Take a few slow, deep breaths. Let your body settle a little bit. Maybe you need to walk away from the dishes and go back to your workstation or outside for a moment. Sometimes, getting away from the trigger of a difficult emotion is important to give us a break.

3. Reflect

Okay, what are your choices here? Do you want to be carrying this irritability into the rest of your day? Did this other person really intend to be annoying? You know that the answer to both questions is "no." What else can you do? You could walk away and leave the dishes for someone else. You could perhaps decide that it is more effective to quickly do them and clear out the sink for yourself and others. In the longer term, you may wish to make a general office announcement to ask for others to be more aware.

4. Choose

In this instance, say you decide that you are going to just work around the dishes and leave them be. You may find that you are tempted to start down an old pathway and post another *larger* note that reminds others again to do their dishes. However, you don't. You stay strong. You feel better already as you let go of judgments and irritation. You soften your thinking as you realize that no one is perfect (yes, not even you) and that behavior change is hard.

Conclusion

The four-step mindfulness is a powerful tool to help us be more aware of the behaviors that we want to change, especially ones that are rooted in emotions. We can use this process to help us slow down and give ourselves the chance to respond as opposed to react to a situation. Automaticity is another important concept to have in mind as you try to act on your new behavior plan when it comes to a difficult emotion. You can have the best of intentions and do your best to be different. Your neurobiology, however, has other plans for you and will be much stronger, especially as you are learning and first implementing new behaviors.

Stay strong and be patient with yourself. Change is difficult, and it is important to have compassion for yourself. How do you practice compassion? I'm glad you asked because that is our focus in the next chapter.

> ### The Least You Need To Know
>
> - Mindfulness is a skill like any other that can be developed with effort.
>
> - Certain emotions can be problematic for us and lead us to act in destructive ways that make situations worse for ourselves and often others.
>
> - Emotions are in fact complicated processes that we can work to understand, especially as we experience them personally.
>
> - The four-step mindfulness helps us to use mindfulness "on the go" in life to deal with stressful situations.
>
> - The four-step mindfulness is an effective strategy to help us more skillfully manage the uncivil behaviors of others.

chapter seven

Compassion:
Searching For Another's Humanity

Who is the person in your life who you find most irritating? I will guess wildly that it is not hard for you to think *immediately* of who that person may be. It may be that you think of *more than one* person. Perhaps it is a neighbor or someone at work. I am sure that you can conjure up numerous candidates for this exercise.

Now I have a newsflash for you. Are you ready? Someone else doing this exercise might have selected *you* as that person. Whaaaat? Nooooo! It is perhaps shocking to realize but there are likely people who find you irritating. Yes, it is true. I will admit that there are people who I find irritating and just do not like. It is not their fault, as they are just being themselves. Nonetheless, I try to limit or avoid contact with them, and I'll tell you about an effective strategy for doing this later in the chapter.

Sources Of Irritation

I was having a conversation with a client recently who was stuck in a deep-seated belief that people at work did not like him. In response to his thought spiral that was getting him more and more depressed, I said something very untherapistlike (if that is even a word—I guess I just made it one). I said to my client, "You are right. People at work don't like you."

He looked at me with wide eyes. Fortunately, I did not stop there. I went on. "Yes, there are likely some people at work who don't like you, and there are some people in the world who don't like you. Guess what? I know that some people in the world don't like me. This is a fact of life." I explained that he was *overestimating* the number of people who disliked him and *underestimating* how others would like him. This has been a difficult belief for him to alter, but we continue to work on it.

Who knew that I would soon learn evidence that would confirm my statements?

When I was the president of Maine Psychological Association, the executive director at the time quipped once that I was the "Energizer Bunny," as I always had a great deal of energy for the organization and activities, which she appreciated. When I finished my term, she awarded me a stuffed animal version of this rabbit.

On the other hand, I recently learned that some clients in our office have nicknames for me, one of which is "Mr. Perky." Apparently, these certain clients find my positive energy *irritating*. I have even had clients find this to be true. I have learned over the years to adjust my demeanor based on the other person, but my baseline mood is upbeat. Some people *just cannot stand* to be around this at all.

Sources Of Anger And Hate

I am going to extend this exploration beyond irritation to intense anger and hate. There have been very few people on this list in my life, but there have been a few. One example would be the neighbors of my widowed aunt, who moved in nearby years ago and seemed very friendly. They offered to help my elderly aunt, who lived alone and presented themselves as compassionate, supportive people. Then, one day, they approached my aunt with plans to renovate their home, which required a "sign-off" from neighbors around them. My aunt was happy to sign this request and support them in creating the home of their dreams. After this document was signed, things changed very quickly.

Once their renovation was approved, these same neighbors suddenly changed their demeanor. It began when the husband pulled his car into my aunt's driveway and blocked her so she could not get out. "We own the driveway. Check your deed. You are parking on our land. From now on, you must park elsewhere."

My aunt had parked her car in the same place for nearly forty years. This began a five-year-long legal battle to remedy a land dispute caused by poorly created deeds in rural Maine in the 1960s.

During this time, the husband began to harass my seventy-five-year-old aunt. He left stern messages on her answering machine about the need to "move her car." He set up a twenty-four-hour-a-day video camera and would frequently take pictures of her going in and out of her house. It was an awful period for our family, especially as this coincided with my mother's other sister slowly dying from breast cancer.

During this time, I was going down to check on my aunt on a regular basis while also serving as the point person for the legal proceedings. As I turned down my aunt's street, I could feel my body tighten as I knew that *I would have to drive by this neighbor's house–I might even see these neighbors out in their yard.*

I would find myself getting intensely angry at the situation, especially since there were few legal remedies to stop their subtle harassment (he was a smart bully who knew how to walk the legal line with what he could get away with). I knew that I had to find some alternate strategy to manage this trigger. The answer would come in a form of compassion.

Compassion And Kindness

"Compassion refers to awareness and feeling for the suffering of others . . . [whereas] empathy encompasses all the feelings of others, not just their struggles."[43] When we are compassionate toward others, we are aware that they have their struggles. We may not know what their struggles are (and we do not necessarily need to know them), but we know that they *do* have difficulties, as we all do in the human condition.

Ancient meditation teachers linked mindfulness and compassion. They noted that these ideas are like "a wing of a bird." A bird needs both wings to soar above the earth. Similarly, a meditator needs mindfulness and an attitude of compassion to be truly grounded and have "affectionate awareness." In short, compassion is an essential component of living with greater awareness.

Some authors see compassion and empathy as fitting under a larger category of kindness. I have read texts that use kindness and compassion interchangeably. Other texts put kindness as an action, whereas compassion is an emotion (that remains internal). For this book's purposes, I will stick with this distinction: compassion is an internal feeling, and kindness is an external action. The good news is that we can benefit from both.

Benefits Of Compassion

You may think we have just taken a hard left at Albuquerque. I was describing this hateful neighbor of my aunt, and I have suddenly switched to writing about kindness. You are now rolling your eyes, thinking that I am going to tell you how I was able to join hands and sing "Kumbaya" with this neighbor just by focusing on compassion for him. Fear not and keep reading, as this is not the end of the story. Just because we can work to feel compassion toward others does not mean that we *must* do so in every situation. It also does not mean that we become doormats.

Compassion For Others
Working to cultivate compassion for others has many general benefits. Compassion can give us a sense of connectedness to others and provide meaning for our lives. It can help create better mental health by reducing risks for psychological distress and increasing the benefits of social support to combat loneliness.[44] Developing compassion for others creates healthy aging and increases longevity in those who volunteer and help others. However, there is another more general benefit of developing compassion: it helps us reorient our brains in a new direction by changing the focus of our motivations.

The more we develop compassion in our brains, the more we are strengthening circuitry that is oriented toward noticing positivity and creating greater contentment. As we have explored previously in this book, our brains are oriented toward survival and therefore they are more likely to notice threat or negativity. Focusing on compassion helps us to shift the balance away from the negative events in our lives to many positive things that happen.

Compassion For Self
As we have established, many people are very good at giving compassion to others and letting go of criticism of others. However, that same sense of compassion is much harder to provide to ourselves. Why? I think that it has to do with our "friendly" internal critic who wants to show up and tell us why things are our fault or how we need to improve. Many of us struggle to feel deserving of self-compassion (except those narcissists, but I believe that deep down, they struggle, too) and find this challenging.

There is a reason to work at self-compassion. Research continues to demonstrate that higher levels of self-compassion have numerous health benefits, some of which include:[45]

- lower levels of depression and anxiety
- lower levels of the stress hormone cortisol
- healthier relationships enhanced by greater empathy, altruism, and forgiveness
- reductions in smoking and increases in exercise and healthy eating

Those who exhibit greater self-compassion are also more likely to have more emotional intelligence, which enhances their ability to regulate their emotions and have more empathy for others.

Benefits Of Kindness

I remember when I first read the research that said that "altruism is not totally altruistic." But wait. How could this be? Altruism is about selflessness in action, or so the belief goes. However, some researchers have concluded that even acts that appear to be selfless provide the doer with self-gratification for being kind. Altruism may serve as a distraction for the doer from their problems or may somehow allow them to feel better about themselves to compensate for some perceived personal weakness. This debate rages on about whether humans can be truly selfless.[46]

Other researchers have explored the relationship between kindness and happiness. Fortunately, there is less debate by psychologists about the relationship between these two concepts. Being kind increases mood-boosting chemicals that occur naturally in our bodies, such as serotonin, dopamine, and endorphins. These neurochemical changes increase areas in the brain controlling pleasure, reward, and mood, leaving the giver of kindness feeling happier. Similar impacts can be seen in the brain of the receiver of kindness. These impacts have mood-boosting effects and lead people to feel happier.[47]

Kindness is also beneficial for social relationships. In his book, *The Five Side Effects of Kindness*, David Hamilton describes how kindness has great benefits for our entire nervous system. Being kind to others generates the "love hormone" oxytocin, which in turn can benefit our hearts by lowering blood pressure and cortisol levels associated with stress. This can lead to happiness in both the giver and the receiver, which can then lead to a greater likelihood of kind acts. Even people who simply witness kind acts can gain similar benefits.[48]

Based on this distinction, kindness is interpersonal (as it is a behavior that others witness) versus compassion, which is *intrapersonal* (as it is a feeling we have internally). For the purposes of this section, I am making recommendations for how to engage in more compassionate self-talk whether focused on self or others. So, without further ado, let's explore how a focus on compassion can help with incivility.

The Compassion Solution: Self

There is an old saying that "the client can only go as far as the therapist has been." This has motivated me throughout my career to try to grow my own self-awareness (it has been a ponderous journey) to be of better help to my clients. Self-awareness is something for all of us to develop.

If you expect civil behavior from others, you must be willing to give that to others, and self-awareness is the necessary foundation to understand our impact on others. In addition, you must be willing to give compassion to yourself, and that is where the process really starts.

Self-Compassion

As noted above, many people find it more challenging to be compassionate with themselves, as compared to other people. Many of my clients struggle with trying to begin their mindfulness journey in this way. Visions come to mind of Stuart Smalley (a character from *Saturday Night Live* many years ago) sitting in front of a mirror saying, "I'm good enough. I'm smart enough. And, doggone it, people like me!"

I have had people roll their eyes or laugh out loud when I start to talk about self-compassion. Likewise, I'm a recovered eye roller (okay, recover-*ing*). When I attend a workshop and the "experiential" component of self-exploration starts, I have the urge to run for the exits. However, I have learned to resist this urge and be open to the experience. Ninety-five percent of the time, I get something from the exercise, and, in some cases, I get a great deal. So, if you are an eye-roller, I invite you to rest your eyes and give this a shot.

Remember that our goal with these activities is to combat our incivility with ourselves. Our goal here is to help you recognize your own negative self-talk that can affect your demeanor and impede your ability to be more grounded in response to the challenges of life and of interacting with others.

Self-Talk To Tame The Critic

Our internal critic has our best interest in mind. When I say this, people get quizzical looks on their faces. Here's what I mean.

Remember the story of Bob the runner that we reviewed earlier in the book? In case you were asleep, here is the essence of that story. "Bob" was running a road race with me and had a running coach (or friend) meet him during the last mile. In an attempt to help him, Bob's coach tried to activate his anger by shaming Bob to "not be a girl" and not allowing me to pass him. The coach's behavior did the opposite, and Bob's performance suffered. It is likely the same for you when your critic shows up.

So, how can you rein in your internal critic?

1. Identify that your internal critic is active—that they are "saying" something in your thoughts. First, note that this is happening.

2. Label your internal critic in some way that you find useful. I call mine "the running coach" (similar to Bob's).

3. Thank your internal critic for what they are doing and let them know that you appreciate their efforts; however, let them know that they can step back as you are going to take it from here (this is where most of the eye-rolling occurs, but I ask people to try it).

4. Replace the negative, critical messages of the critic with messages of compassion. Is this hard to create for yourself? Think about someone in your past or present life whom you find to be very compassionate. This may be a person in your life previously or now (grandmother, pastor, teacher, coach). It also may be a famous person or religious figure (angel, Dalai Lama, Christ) who represents compassion to you and whom you might see as a resource.

5. Imagine that this person is sitting beside you now. Perhaps you can imagine them speaking these messages of support to you. You might also imagine that this person has a hand on your shoulder as you repeat these messages to yourself. Do what works for you.

6. Now, take a few minutes to gently repeat compassionate messages to yourself. Some examples might be: "You can do this" or "You are okay."

I remember one client in particular who was a frequent eye-roller in our sessions. I introduced this idea in one meeting, and it was met with the expected eye movement. To her credit, she sighed and said, "Okay, I'll try it."

She returned to our next session and reported with a grin, "Okay, I'll admit it. *You were right!* It worked." I smiled and asked her to repeat this, "Wait, who was right?" We both had a good laugh, and I was surprised that it worked for her. So, maybe there is hope for you?

Hand Over Heart Exercise

I am going to summarize this exercise here, which I have learned from several sources. I was first exposed to it in reading Terry Fralich's book, *The Five Core Skills of Mindfulness*, and thought that it could provide a great foundation for developing self-compassion.[49] Here is my summary of this exercise:

1. Find a comfortable position to sit or lie down and close your eyes. If you are more comfortable with eyes open, focus your gaze on something in front of you or across the room from you that can be a focus but not a distraction. (For example, maybe you can focus on the wall or a piece of furniture as opposed to a TV or computer screen with ever-changing images that could be a distraction.) If you start to feel any significant distress, you can try to "let it go by like scenery on a train." If that does not work, do not stay with this distress. Distract yourself with something else (such as music or calling a friend to talk about something else).

2. Begin by taking a few deep breaths. Let your body relax. Next, put one or both hands over your heart and let them just settle there. Notice how that feels. Continue breathing.

3. Think about a time in your life when you offered comfort or compassion to someone else (such as a child or friend in distress). As you think about this instance, notice what you feel in your body and allow yourself to pay attention to that for as long as you feel comfortable.

4. Next, choose a phrase or phrases that provide you with comfort and that help you to counter the negative messages you might get caught up in when your "running coach" is berating you about your latest mistake. Some ideas might be:

You are okay.

You are safe.

You are loved.

5. Now, repeat the phrase(s) you chose above while holding your hands on your heart. Once again, some people will do well with holding their hands over their heart and repeating the phrases noted above. Other people may do better by just focusing on the body and sitting/lying down with their hands over their heart. This position may be comforting enough as a nonverbal message of self-compassion.

So, the next time you catch yourself being critical or negative about yourself, try the exercises above. A lack of compassion for yourself can lead you to feel irritable or angry. These emotions can leak out in both direct and indirect uncivil behaviors toward others. The Golden Rule, "Treat others as you wish to be treated," is relevant here. You cannot expect behavior from others toward you that you are not willing to provide to others.

The Compassion Solution: Others

Compassion for others may be easier or more difficult, depending on who you are. For most of my clients, this form of compassion is easier. However, notice that I did *not* say easy, but easier. There are many challenges to approaching relationships with other people with compassion, especially when they are being uncivil toward us.

Some of you out there are thinking, "John, *why* would we *even try* to be compassionate toward those other people? They are treating us so poorly and you want us to just 'turn the other cheek?' Are we to be doormats?" Cue the Kumbaya.

No, I am not suggesting that you call upon the skills of compassion to benefit others. You don't have to do anything for the benefit of someone who is acting inappropriately. Rather, compassion is for *your* benefit. Yes, *your* benefit. Now, do I have your attention?

There is an old saying credited to Saint Augustine that goes like this: "Resentment is like drinking poison and then waiting for the other person to die." I have morphed this statement into my own version. "Resentment is the poison I drink, thinking that it will harm you."

Carrying around resentments against other people will not affect them unless they are acted upon, and most people don't do that. They simply let their feelings of resentment fester inside, and this can affect their health. Remember the bumper sticker from earlier, "Your hate becomes you." It is so very true. Let's look at some solutions.

Loving Kindness Meditation

1. Once again, find a comfortable position to sit or lie down and close your eyes. If you are more comfortable with eyes open, focus your gaze on something in front of you or across the room from you that can be a focus but not a distraction. Reminder: If you start to feel any significant distress, you can try to "let it go by like scenery on a train." If that does not work, do not stay with this distress. Distract yourself with something else.

2. Once again, begin by taking a few deep breaths. Let your body relax. Next, put one or both hands over your heart and let them just settle there. Notice how that feels. Continue breathing.

3. Next, repeat the following phrases slowly and pause in between each phrase.

    May you be happy.

    May you be healthy.

    May you be free from suffering.

    May you live a safe and gentle life.

    (pause)

4. The general pattern for this meditation is to start by sending loving kindness to yourself and then to others in a prescribed pattern. After focusing on yourself, you send loving kindness to a loved one/friend, then to a person in your life who you don't know well (neutral person), then to a difficult person, and finally to all sentient beings.

When dealing with incivility from others, you may find it beneficial to limit your use of the various levels to the first four. Some people find it too difficult at first to show loving kindness to difficult people. Start wherever you can because focusing on compassion in general and this type of meditation can help shift your brain.

Gently Avoiding, AKA "Adaptive Shunning"

"Shunning" is behavior that ignores the existence of another person. It has its roots in a variety of cultures. The Amish are known for shunning people who leave the community or who are determined by the leaders to have violated the rules. Once this determination is made, members of the community are not allowed to speak to this person, not a word. If the person, for whatever reason, must stay in the vicinity of others but not be able to interact with anyone, this act of being shunned has negative effects on their health, including an early death or "dying of loneliness."

My people (Irish Americans) are also known for engaging in this behavior. I remember family stories about previous generations attending holiday gatherings where some siblings weren't speaking to each other at the time. They would both attend and act as if the other did not exist. Although they were acting like the other was not there, naturally, they knew that they were there, and they were *acting* on their resentments toward the other person. In addition to the complications for those siblings involved in shunning, this situation presented many challenges for others present.

So, now, I am suggesting that you use *shunning* to deal with those people who are uncivil toward you. Some of you are very excited. *Yes!* We will *show them*. We will send a message to them that they will never forget!

Before you get too excited about this, I will remind you of the title of this skill: *adaptive shunning*. In this version of shunning, no one gets hurt, neither you nor the other person. Instead, you are gently avoiding or ignoring the person and doing your best to just not engage with them. It is shunning without the resentment or passive-aggressiveness of trying to "send a message" to the other. It is recognizing that others are simply being themselves or perhaps acting out of emotions or dynamics that have nothing to do with us. How does this work?

Let's return to the scenario I described earlier in the chapter: my aunt's uncivil neighbors. I will readily admit that this was a *major challenge* in trying to use skills to manage my reactions. If someone is picking on a family member of ours, we will naturally have the urge to come to the defense of our loved one. Now add in that it is your aunt, who is elderly and living alone about an hour away from you with neighbors who are actively engaging in bullying and harassing behaviors. Baseball has a World Series that crowns the championship team for that year. Dealing with these neighbors was like the World Series of mindfulness.

Other mindfulness experts might tell you that they could do the "Loving Kindness" meditation for these people daily without batting an eyelash. Good for them. For me, other strategies of compassion were simply not possible. That left me with one option that I thought I could use: adaptive shunning.

This starts with trying to "step back" inside and reflect on how the other person's behavior is not about you. In this case, I learned that the husband of this duo was on his third marriage, and she was on her second. He had a reputation in the neighborhood for having a temper and, at times, could be heard yelling.

Based on this limited information, I surmised that they did not have an easy relationship. I thought about how difficult it would be to be either of these people. This helped me to unhook from reacting to their behavior and feeling as if it was personal toward me.

When I turned onto my aunt's street, I purposefully took a few deep breaths. I intentionally avoided looking at the neighbor's house as I drove down the street into her driveway. While visiting my aunt, I kept my focus away from the neighbors' house and focused on other beautiful things in the area. On occasion, my eyes would drift over to their house, especially if one of them was in the yard. I would gently bring my focus back to other things.

The end of this story is that, eventually, the lawsuit was settled. While she did not get all that we hoped she would get, she was able to get clear boundaries and some financial compensation from them for damages to her property. Once the lawsuit ended, these neighbors had to put their house up for sale as they were divorcing. Living in anger can have consequences on our personal relationships, even if our anger is not about them.

The moral of the story is this: sometimes the best thing to do in response to someone's behavior is nothing. The more that you engage with them, the more potential problems can emerge. We will talk about an interpersonal strategy that you can also use in tandem with this internal one to manage your desire to engage and "fight for your rights."

Conclusion

Compassion can be an important tool to use in response to uncivil behavior from others. I hope that this chapter has shown you how this tool works and how it can be of benefit to you. Stop drinking the "resentment Kool-Aid" and free yourself from this toxicity. Your body will be grateful that you did.

> ### The Least You Need To Know
>
> - Despite our best efforts, we are not going to like everyone on the planet, and they will not all like us.
>
> - Compassion refers to our ability to reflect on the struggles and difficulties that others may have as we interact with them.
>
> - Growing our ability to use compassion has potential benefits for others and ourselves.
>
> - We can learn specific meditation strategies to help us develop our abilities for a compassionate approach to others and ourselves.
>
> - Sometimes, the most effective way to engage with others is to not engage with them at all.

chapter eight

Grounding:
How To "Care Less"

I can remember the day of the meeting as if it were yesterday. I worked for Jackson Brook Institute, a local psychiatric hospital, in my first job following my doctoral program. To become fully licensed after completing their degree, psychologists must work for an additional year under somebody else's supervision. Jackson Brook served as a primary provider for a continuum of mental health and substance abuse services in Maine. This hospital was seemingly thriving and was a highly respected organization in the local area, expanding programming and opening offices throughout the southern part of the state of Maine while hiring staff rapidly. Life was good, and things seemed very hopeful.

However, it was not long before things quickly took a turn for the worse. Apparently, the owners had been too aggressive in their growth plans, and suddenly, there was not enough funding to cover all the programs. Programs closed, and staff were laid off. There wasn't enough money to cover each week's payroll. Meanwhile, we had to provide good care for our clients while wondering if we could cash our paychecks—or even have jobs tomorrow.

Our immediate bosses handled this time of chaos and frustration with the utmost professionalism and support. My boss's boss would show up randomly in the morning with bagels for all of us. She offered her support. She also provided regular meetings to keep us up to date on all that she knew.

During one of these meetings, the discussion began to circle back to the circumstances that led to Jackson Brook's problems. One of my colleagues asked the same questions that she had asked in the meetings over the last three days. She offered the same comments and went on a soliloquy about how unfair this all was and how she thought the problems started in the first place.

I could feel my irritation rising. *"You are saying the same thing that you have said for three days in a row. Are you expecting different results?"* The longer she talked, the more I was able to predict her next word or phrase. It was like we were reading from the same script.

Fortunately, I was already somewhat aware of how to use my skills when this meeting occurred. I thought to myself that the only chance I had to get away from this irritation was *grounding* and that this was a perfect opportunity to use it. What is grounding? How is it something that could be helpful in a situation like this? Let me explain.

Grounding

As I began conducting research for this book, I learned that "grounding" can refer to different techniques, including connecting to the healing energies of the earth by lying down or walking barefoot.[50]

The type of grounding to which I am referring is a different, though related, type of grounding. Grounding, as I think about it, is a strategy that has been used by people who have experienced trauma or other mental health distress. You may remember in the chapter on breathing I indicated that not

> everybody could benefit from breathing because some people become highly anxious when they focus on their body, and they begin to feel very unsafe. These people have an alternative strategy to focus themselves away from the body in a way that is more effective. This involves grounding to their environment—or some other aspect of experience *away* from the body.

Grounding's Purpose

The purpose of grounding is to *disrupt* our current focus and to *distract us* onto something else.[51] Unlike mindfulness strategies that want us to focus more deeply into our experience, grounding gets us to direct our attention *away* from our current experience. The idea of these skills is to help us escape from something distressing that threatens to dominate our experience and lead to problematic behavior.

One of the most painful parts of experiencing disturbing memories of a traumatic incident and post-traumatic stress disorder (PTSD) is how a survivor's world can suddenly be turned upside down with reminders of the event(s). A sight or sound can trigger memories for survivors in ways that are not always or not at all predictable. Grounding is one strategy that can be of help to trauma survivors as they seek to heal.[52]

Even though you may not have experienced trauma, your life can also be disrupted by emotional pain. A difficult emotion or memory can come into your mind and affect you in the moment. Sometimes, those disturbing associations can be related to events happening right then. However, you can also be reacting to things that happened an hour ago, a day ago, or ten years ago that enter your mind and threaten to dominate your experience. These painful memories/associations can leave you feeling "off balance," and therefore, you are more likely to act in uncivil ways. Grounding can be the solution to help you keep from reacting in ways that you may later regret.

Factors To Remember

When using grounding skills, we need to be aware of many variables that are an important context for grounding. This list is not exhaustive, and I would encourage you to review additional materials on grounding (including the work of Dr. Lisa Najavits, *Seeking Safety*[53]) if you decide that you want to use this strategy as a foundational skill for coping. Keep in mind the following ideas:

Grounding is not relaxation. Grounding and relaxation are two different things. Relaxation is about focusing the body on releasing tension and allowing physical sensations to soften and "let go." Grounding is a more active and engaged approach to the moment wherein you work to direct your attention to some specific aspect of your experience. Some people find relaxation "too passive," preferring the "active" approach to the environment that grounding provides.

Focus away from the painful image/event. The goal of grounding is to direct attention away from the painful circumstance. Many people find comfort in journaling or drawing to release feelings. If these strategies work for you, keep using them. However, if you are grounding, your focus needs to be on things other than the source of irritation. For example, if, as you are going into a meeting, you are irritated by something that a colleague has just said to you (and this person is going to be in the meeting), try to position yourself away from this person and perhaps in a part of the room where they are out of your visual field.

Eyes open. People often close their eyes when they are trying to relax and refocus. Some people close their eyes to do deep breathing so that they can be as focused on their physical being as possible. If you wish to do a relaxation strategy, closing your eyes may work for you.

When it comes to grounding, you want to keep your eyes open. Some of the strategies that I will suggest will require you to be examining aspects of your physical environment. In addition, vision helps you to stay attuned to your present surroundings. With your eyes closed, you can easily fall back into thoughts or feelings associated with the source of your irritation. Eyes open will give you a better chance of being here now.

Being nonjudgmental. We have reviewed the importance of being nonjudgmental elsewhere in this book, so I am going to simply remind you of its use. When we are nonjudgmental, we are focused on facts, not feelings. We try to describe things (ourselves or others) in ways that avoid labels of things like bad, stupid, lazy, or incompetent. When you try grounding, work to let go of criticism and just do the best that you can.

Categories Of Grounding

Different authors may organize grounding skills in various ways. As you already know, I am a huge fan of the work of Dr. Lisa Najavits. In her book *Seeking Safety*, she instructs people to choose from strategies in three major categories: mental, physical, and soothing.[54]

Mental

Mental grounding is about choosing to put something in your mind so that thoughts about the distressing event do not have the opportunity to continue to build in your mind. When we are upset and try to direct our attention elsewhere, our attention is still naturally drawn back to the person or situation that is upsetting us. We tell ourselves, "I cannot think about that. I need to think about anything else but that."

Try something for me in this moment. Please do not think about pink elephants. Keep pink elephants out of your mind. Think about anything else except pink elephants.

So, how successful were you? If you are like most of us (there are always exceptions to every rule), you kept thinking about pink elephants. As we try to remind ourselves not to think about something, we are reminding ourselves of that something, which then reinforces this topic and grows its strength. Try instead to pick your mind up and put it onto something else. Ideas for mental grounding include:

- *Describe something in your environment* in detail by studying its appearance carefully in your mind (spoiler alert: I am going to give you an example of this later in this chapter).
- *Complete a word search or crossword puzzle.* Friends of mine are hooked on the New York Times game called "Wordle." If you enjoy word puzzles, I highly recommend it.
- *Funny things.* Go into a store and read the funny birthday cards (even if you are not looking to buy). You can also watch funny videos online. I enjoy watching the latest cat or dog videos for distraction and humor.
- *Counting.* Count back from one hundred to one very slowly. I had a boss who used this skill to get to sleep each night. She swore by it and never got past the seventies.
- *Meditation or prayer.* People in recovery from addiction and others may use "The Serenity Prayer." Other mantras or meditations are also available. Find something that holds your attention.

Physical

Some people find that their stress is created primarily in their heads as they churn on the stressor in their minds repeatedly. For those people, mental grounding will likely be the most effective skill. Other people hold tension in their bodies, and this tightness becomes the primary breeding ground for irritation and tension, which builds and builds. In this case, a physical grounding technique might be of use. Some of my favorites include:

- *Cold water.* You can run your hands under cold water or splash cold water on your face. In the past few years, I have coaxed clients to do this in the middle of a session when they were getting particularly stressed. This has worked like a charm in virtual sessions, too, as people often feel more comfortable doing this in their home environment.

- *Feet on the floor.* Put your feet flat on the floor and focus on the sensations of where your foot meets the floor or the bottom of your shoe (or bunny slipper). Work to bring your full and complete attention to these sensations. You may find it helpful to dig your heels into the floor to help bring your awareness to this part of your body. If you are standing, you can rock back and forth, pressing down on your left, then your right, then your left, and so on. I have used this strategy when I am about to speak publicly and am experiencing a sudden rush of anxiety.

- *Mindful walking.* Bring your attention to the process of walking. If you can walk very slowly, focus on every aspect of your movement. Notice as the heel of your foot hits the ground and then as your foot rolls forward until you are on the toe of that foot. Notice as your weight shifts onto the other foot, and the process continues.

- *Dance.* Yes, dance. Now, this strategy will not work effectively in all environments, especially if you are in the office. However, if you are somewhere by yourself, you can put on music that you love and move your body.

- *Stretch.* In recent years, I have tried to be much more cognizant of the tension that I am carrying in my body. I had a bout with severe back pain in my upper back and neck years ago and learned that I needed to be more aware of how I was holding tension. You can easily stretch almost any place, even stretching your legs under the table in a difficult meeting (just be careful not to kick your colleague). Stretching in various ways can feel good and give you something physical to have as a focus.

Soothing

So many of us are our own worst critics. If we are not careful, we can find ourselves repeating negative thoughts about ourselves. I ask people, "What would you do if someone called you and was saying those awful things to you?" People look at me quizzically and say, "Well, *of course I would hang up*." I then tell them to think about doing the same thing with their internal critic.

Sometimes, the internal negative messages are more about how unbearable the situation is or how unprepared the person is to deal with it. These messages once again only make a difficult situation even worse. Use soothing strategies to be gentler and more compassionate with yourself in that moment. Some options for soothing strategies could be the following:

- *Internal cheerleader.* Imagine that an internal cheerleader replaced your internal critic. What would your cheerleader say? I had a colleague in graduate school who *had been* a cheerleader (so I trust her recommendations), and she used the following cheer to get herself through hard times. This is said in a fast-paced rhythm:

    "You can do it, you can do it, you can!"

    "You can do it, you can do it, you can!"

    "You can do it, you can do it, if you set your mind to it!"

    "You can do it, you can do it, you can!"

- *Soothing statement/song.* This statement may be something as simple as "You are okay." or "Take it one step at a time." Some people find comfort in using a religious statement or the name of a religious figure to help them. People may also find comfort in songs. I have found great solace in using comforting songs to listen to or sing to myself as I faced painful moments in my life, including when my father lay dying.

- *Favorite things.* I can hear Julie Andrews singing the song "My Favorite Things" in *The Sound of Music*. "Raindrops on roses and whiskers on kittens…" Maria (her character in the story) apparently was ahead of her time in cajoling the von Trapp family children to use soothing grounding. The last line of the song goes, "I simply remember my favorite things, and then I don't feel so bad."[55] Try it for yourself.

- *People you care about.* Take a moment to picture people you care about and perhaps you know care about you. I have many clients who are parents and who keep pictures of their kids in their wallets or on their phones. Don't have children? I bet that you have relatives or friends. For many people, their dog/cat/fish/salamander or other pet is a source of happiness. Pull out a picture. If you are home with those people, go seek them out and hug them (if they are in the mood to be hugged).

- *Smells.* This idea could also be considered physical. Are there flowers in your home or office that please you? Do you love to burn candles or incense? If this describes you, consider how you enjoy scents that soothe you.

Application

So, back to the scene where I was trapped in a distressing meeting. When we left off in our story, I was in a meeting with my colleagues, feeling the increasing likelihood that we wouldn't have jobs the following day or week. I was also at that moment trying to contain my frustration, listening as I was to my colleague repeat the *exact* same questions and make the *exact* same points that she had made in previous days. Even those of us with long fuses can have a limit. I was clearly at mine.

As my colleague continued her soliloquy, I looked across the large table at her and tried to breathe deeply without anyone noticing. This strategy wasn't working, and I was afraid to do it with any more vim and vigor as it would "let the cat out of the bag" about the fact that I was implementing a relaxation strategy. I was in a room full of clinicians who could spot stress a mile away.

I could feel my irritation building. "Yikes! I think that my face is turning red. Quick, John, do something. Do something! DEFCON 5! Implement emergency measures!"

We have beautiful autumn foliage in Maine, and people come from miles around and from faraway places to witness the beauty that we have all around us daily. If you have never visited northern New England during autumn, I encourage you to add this to your "bucket list" of "must-sees" in life.

Suddenly, I saw it. Just behind my colleague, it was in full view: a tree that had just reached its peak foliage color of a beautiful orange. I began to scan the leaves of this tree and noticed all the variations and shades of orange that were contained in this one tree. I marveled at its beauty and soon found myself focused on the details of each leaf. I found myself feeling grateful that I had the opportunity to see this. How had I not noticed this before? My thoughts became focused on the joy and wonder of witnessing a thing of beauty that nature creates for us each year.

It was like changing the channel on TV from a show that you despise to an old relaxing movie or sitcom that you enjoy. I could feel myself becoming more relaxed, and my blood was no longer headed for a full rolling boil. Although I did keep one ear focused on the discussion in the meeting, just to be sure that I was not called upon or that a topic change had occurred, I was physically transported to a different state. I felt much calmer and more relaxed.

> It was like changing the channel on TV from a show that you despise to an old relaxing movie or sitcom that you enjoy.

Conclusion

Unlike other skills that you will learn, grounding has the purpose of disrupting the current moment and pushing your attention elsewhere. This skill can be of help for people who find that they are not able to use deep breathing to calm themselves successfully.

We reviewed the three major categories that I use when I talk about or practice grounding myself: mental, physical, and soothing. Find what works for you and work to practice it regularly when you don't need it. You will be grateful that you did when the "you-know-what" hits the fan.

The Least You Need To Know

- Grounding can be a very effective strategy in purposefully disrupting what we are thinking or feeling and allowing us to focus more fully on something else.

- Grounding is different from relaxation and is about actively engaging with aspects of the environment around you.

- When we use grounding, we keep our eyes open and focus away from the source of our pain or discomfort (whether physical or emotional).

- We approach grounding ideally nonjudgmentally, without labeling our efforts as "good enough" or "done correctly." It is about trying without "grading" how well we are doing it.

- Mental, physical, and soothing grounding all involve different strategies to change our focus. By exploring all these strategies, you can find what works for you.

PART 3

Reclaiming Civility With Others

chapter nine

WAIT:
Why Am I Talking?

My parents took my sister and me to a local arcade when I was six. We were given a limited supply of quarters, which we could use at our discretion. I was convinced that great winnings awaited me at the Skee-Ball machines, where you roll a ball up into a maze and aim to win prizes (the greatest of which was that *huge* stuffed animal on display). I blew all my quarters on these machines in the blink of an eye and, unfortunately, came away empty-handed, not winning even the smallest trinkets.

On the other hand, my sister decided to diversify her use of quarters across a much wider array of machines and games. She played several different games, and although she did not get a prized stuffed animal, she enjoyed the variety of sights and sounds these games provided. Down to her last quarter, she decided that the magical fortune teller machine was to be its recipient.

She made her way across the arcade over to the machine, deposited the quarter, and then stood back, eyes wide with anticipation. Inside, several lights blinked in rhythm while a mysterious animated figure gyrated back and forth several times before spitting out life-changing advice on a small card. My sister stood and awaited guidance about what to do with her life.

I want to take a moment here to explain the context of what happened next. My sister, Carol, is five-and-a-half years older to the day than I am. In school, she was six years ahead of me. This meant that there was a large gap between us, long enough for teachers to ideally forget the last name and to allow me to create my own path—or so I thought.

On the first day of school, every year, the scenario would be the same. The nun would call my name and then say, "O'Brien, you have a sister, Carol Ann, right?" (I would nod in agreement, trying to adhere to the *rule of quiet*). "She talked too much. Don't follow in her footsteps. Now sit down." Every year, these events would unfold with great predictability.

Yes, in fact, my sister loved to talk and be social (and still does), sometimes apparently to the detriment of the nun's lesson plan. Truth be told, she went on to become a stellar teacher herself, where she now gets to talk in her classroom as much as she wants.

Now, let's go back to our story from many years ago. My sister was waiting before the machine, eyes wide in anticipation and excitement, to find her path to the future based on the sage advice from the fortune teller. The machine stopped gyrating and spit out her fortune in the form of a white card. She picked up the card with great glee and eagerly read the important message. I still remember it to this day:

> *The wise old owl, sat in an oak*
> *The more he listened, the less he spoke*
> *The less he spoke, the more he heard*
> *Why can't you be like that wise old bird?*

The skill I am going to teach you in this chapter could be summarized by this sage advice from the fortune teller. In short, sometimes it is best not to talk but to just listen and be quiet. In fact, there can be great skill and power in this response. Although it is not always the best way to react, it can sometimes be the most effective choice. Let me tell you how.

> In short, sometimes it is best not to talk but to just listen and be quiet.

Silence

Unless you are a hermit (which I doubt you would be if you had gotten your hands on this book), you are faced with some noise in your life. For most of us, our lives are filled with a range of constant stimulation, from nature's sounds and the voices of other humans to the cacophony of sounds heard by those living in larger urban areas.

We can develop some reduced reactivity to noise through a process known as sensory adaptation, whereby our bodies learn to reduce our awareness of a stimulus.[56] I live near both the airport and train station in Portland, Maine. The loudness of planes landing can sometimes shock friends who are visiting. The train whistle for the 5 a.m. trip to Boston can rouse some guests from their sleep. I rarely, if ever, hear any of these noises and have pushed them to the background in my awareness.

Many people, however, are not as easily able to "tune out" environmental noises. I think of one client who struggles with noise adaptation. Whenever a fire truck or police car goes by the office during our session, my client stops and winces. He cannot continue with our conversation until this sound subsides. Being able to tune into important sounds and tune out ones that are not important is the phenomenon known as selective attention. Some of us are better able to use this skill than others. Those who cannot are more easily bothered by extraneous environmental noises.

You may be reading this and thinking that putting so much attention on noise is not necessary. In fact, noise was first identified as a public health issue in the late 1960s, originally in developed countries and most primarily in larger cities. Transportation, construction, and machinery were all sources of economic development but also significant noise. Noise is a current target for public health due to connections between noise and health conditions such as high blood pressure, cardiac problems, sleep disturbance, and overall higher stress levels.[57]

Why am I telling you this? Think about the implications of this for incivility. More stress and disturbed sleep will create the perfect storm for reduced patience and a greater risk of incivility. Those who live or work in more densely populated urban environments, as well as those whose job involves loud noise, will be more at risk for this phenomenon.

So, noise is not good for us, and we experience its negative impact. Therefore, we must love silence, right? Even though silence has many benefits, we also have a complicated relationship with it, and many of us want to do whatever we can to mitigate it.

Benefits Of Reduced Noise

Research shows that when we dial down the noise, we dial up many health benefits for ourselves. Silence can be a way to combat hypertension, also known as the silent killer, which is marked by high blood pressure and is a disease that affects nearly half of the American population. Recent research has demonstrated promising results on how just two minutes of silence can reduce heart rate and blood pressure levels.[58] Notice that—just two minutes.

I will sometimes do two-minute mindfulness exercises with clients, and they always remark on how much calmer they feel in a short amount of time. This research simply confirms something that my clients already tell me experientially.

Research continues to explore the many potentials of taking pauses to be quiet. Here are some of the other benefits of silence for our health:[59]

- *Reduced cortisol.* Cortisol is a hormone associated with stress. As stress levels climb, so do our cortisol levels. Over time, higher cortisol can contribute to sleep disturbance, weight gain, and a host of other chronic illnesses.
- *Stimulated brain growth.* Research with mice has shown that two hours of silence activates nerve cell growth in brain areas related to memory function. I realize that there is a big leap from mice to humans, but this does make sense intuitively, as silence is also related to improvements in creative thinking.
- *Better sleep.* This is more of an indirect effect. However, having some quiet times during the day seems to be related to better sleep at night. Who knew that Mrs. Cochran (my kindergarten teacher) was right when she sent us off to our mats to "rest quietly" for a few minutes?

Drawbacks Of Reduced Noise

Silence is not always as "golden," as the oft-quoted proverb may say. We have just explored the many benefits of silence, which are all true. However, there are drawbacks to being silent as well. Some of the perceptions and misperceptions of silence include:

- *Lack of knowledge.* In Western cultures, silence in response to a question or comment can be perceived as ignorance or lack of knowledge, which can reflect poorly on individuals who are not responding.

- *Agreement.* When people do not respond to a speaker, that individual may perceive that others agree. There are also stories of bosses asking for "feedback" from employees about a change and assuming that all were in favor when no one spoke up. Workers may feel that this situation is a "done deal" and that their input is meaningless.

- *Anger.* Some people can misread silence from someone as the "silent treatment" meant to communicate anger. This can be perceived as acting on resentment in ineffective ways that we have explored elsewhere in the book.

- *Lack of power.* Sometimes, not responding to someone gives them the upper hand. I have been the target of insensitive or nasty comments in a group, whether in person or online. While my initial response may have been silence, I eventually found a way to respond (not react) to demonstrate that I would not be intimidated or bullied. In another example, one of my clients was in a conflict with someone, and a friend of his told him, "You are being pulled into a knife fight, and you have a slipper in your hand." Sometimes, you must match force of some kind with equal force to regain your power.

This list is not comprehensive, but I wanted to show you the counterpoint to the idea that silence is a good thing. While it is a useful strategy in what I am about to describe, it is not always *the* strategy to use. That is why it is so important when dealing with incivility that you decide what is most effective for you in that moment and whether to respond or not.

Silence And Discomfort

Anglophones (English speakers) are the world's leaders, aren't we? Well, we often like to think so, and we may use this belief when we travel abroad. In my travels, I have witnessed many Americans in Europe who think that simply speaking English *more s-l-o-w-l-y* and *loudly* will help them communicate with the locals. It is times like this that I tuck my American passport deeper into my pocket. If you learn nothing else from this book, remember this: *the world does not revolve around America.*

However, English speakers (Americans and others) are the true leaders in the world regarding a few things, including discomfort with silence. We are accustomed to having only very short gaps during discussions with others. We generally leave just a few milliseconds of conversational space as we take turns interacting with others. As time gaps lengthen, our discomfort levels increase. Research has shown that once we get to a four-second gap in conversation, we begin to feel increasingly unsettled and want to say something to make it end.[60]

In contrast, speakers of other languages are more tolerant of silence and, in fact, welcome it. Asian and Nordic cultures are thought to be "listening cultures" wherein it is seen as a sign that those involved are pausing to engage in careful reflection. In meetings, Japanese businessmen were found to be comfortable with at least eight seconds or more of silence, at least twice that of Anglophones.[61]

This is an English speaker's Achilles' heel and is well-known worldwide. This serves as a distinct disadvantage in negotiations internationally as business leaders hammer out the details of contracts. English speakers will do well to work to embrace the power and benefits of silence.

Silence As A Response To Incivility

My mom taught my sister and me many important life skills as we grew up. One of those lessons is summarized in the following way: "If you can't say anything nice, don't say anything at all." I have passed this wisdom along to my German friends and done my best to translate the sentiment: *"Sei nett oder sag nichts."* (Literal translation: be nice or say nothing.) I have helped these friends learn how different our cultures are regarding the level of directness and how important it is for them to adjust this when speaking English.

I wish that I could say that I have followed my mom's advice all the time. Well, I could say that, but it would not be the truth. There have been many times in my life when I have replied to someone else's comment and soon regretted what I said. Sometimes, the best response to incivility is nothing at all.

I bet that you are wondering, "How do we know when it is best to say nothing versus when it is best to reply to defend ourselves?" While I cannot give you a flow chart or decision tree, I can offer you my thoughts on things to consider for when it might be best to say nothing:

- *When the source of incivility is not credible.* I was speaking with a client recently who described someone who was on social media making nasty posts about my client's business. "What should I do?" he asked me. When we discussed this further, he described this person as having a reputation for posting nasty things about businesses in his area all day, every day. (Good grief.) I advised my client to do nothing as his business did not depend on social media, and this person was "the boy who cried wolf" locally, whom people were no longer considering credible.

- *When replying is going to pull you further into a mud-slinging brawl.* This can be related to the previous item, and in the case of my client, it was. He described how this person was known for drawing people into public exchanges in meetings or on social media that would devolve into hateful and demeaning exchanges. We even see this at the national level in politics and how some politicians seem to enjoy engaging in outrageous rhetoric to boost their national visibility.

- *When you are not sure how much support you have in the moment.* You may be in a new group of people, and you are not sure if you are with allies or those who will agree with the uncivil person.

- *When you are not at your best.* There are just some days that we are not at our best. In the recovery world, people remember the acronym HALT: Hungry, Angry, Lonely, Tired. This shorthand reminds people that these emotional and physical conditions can create emotional vulnerability wherein people are less capable of responding effectively and are more likely to react. I encourage my clients to be aware of their own physical and emotional state. On days when they are "off," I advise them not to make any major decisions if they are not required to do so.

- *When you are at work.* You may have the perfect witty and sarcastic comment to *reply all* to that email from your coworker to your team in which he said something about you. You find yourself typing it out with glee and want to *show him* that you are better and that you are "not going to take it lying down." However, before you hit the "send" button, *stop*. Remember, your behavior reflects on no one else but you, regardless of what other people are saying or doing. Even if it feels good in the moment, your "slam" of someone else may come back to haunt you at your annual review or in your application for a promotion to leadership. It may be best to just not reply.

The Skill Of WAIT

Now, we get to the core skill that is the focus of this chapter. Drum roll, please. This skill is summarized by the acronym WAIT. W-A-I-T.

I am not the creator of this skill, and I am not sure to whom I should be offering credit. However, I loved this skill as soon as I learned about it and offer it to you as an important tool in your toolkit when dealing with others who are uncivil.

There is no great mystery to this skill as it stands for a simple acronym:

Why

Am

I

Talking?

How is this skill effective when it comes to social interactions with others? How can you use this skill to deal with incivility? I think of two ways specifically:

- *Before you talk.* This option would change the acronym in a way that is less snazzy from its original version to WAIWTT—Why Am I Wanting To Talk? This is less compelling, so I suggest that you keep the original acronym but apply it with the understanding that you are *keeping* yourself from speaking. Think of the examples that I just mentioned above. Maybe you are in an interaction with a source that is not credible, and so you say nothing in reply.

- *Once you have started talking.* This version is for those of us who find ourselves starting to speak before we fully realize that we have done so. You hear a voice replying in a situation, and suddenly it comes to you, "Eek, that is me!" In this case, the "horse is out of the barn," so your choice is a different one. Think to yourself, "What am I doing? Is this really effective right now?" If the answer is "no," then *stop* talking as soon as you can.

WAIT. This acronym and the skill sound so simple that they must be easy to implement, correct? Not necessarily. As noted above, we in the United States are a society that feels great discomfort with silence, and we want to leap in to fill it. This was the trap that I fell into in the following story, which recounts a time early in my career when it would have been more effective to *say nothing*.

What *Not* To Do

I started my career as a high school guidance counselor. I grew immensely during those two years with the support and mentoring of the other members of the guidance department. I was working in the high school of a very wealthy community that took pride each year in touting the acceptance rate of graduating seniors at some of the nation's most competitive colleges and universities. Parents in the community were highly anxious to repeat their "streak" each year, and many were deeply concerned when I, a new graduate, was hired into a position that could affect the trajectory of their children's lives forever.

It was May of my second year, and I was sitting in our task force meeting, a mix of faculty and parents. There were about twenty members in the room, and the discussion that day focused on how to manage the student alcohol use that occurs around prom and graduation. The meeting was about fifteen minutes from ending when the following happened.

"Tammy" (not her real name) raised her hand, and the facilitator recognized her. Tammy was a parent whose children attended schools in the district. Her oldest child, "Barry" (again, not his real name to protect the innocent), was a very bright and highly motivated student. Barry was in my office at least weekly to drop by and "chat" or just "hang out" for a few minutes when my door was open. I provided him with help as he navigated the minefield that is adolescent social dynamics. I had spent time supporting Tammy, too. We had talked about his transition to school in the first year I was there. In my second year, we would check in briefly about his progress at the beginning or end of each task force meeting. I also had two meetings with her during the year about his academic progress, which was stellar. He was adjusting well to the school and developing good social skills. Barry was not a kid to worry about.

"I have something to say," Tammy said at the meeting. She proceeded to go on a rant about the guidance department and how "closed off" and "inaccessible" we were. "You can never get any information out of that department. I have been completely shut out, and other parents say the same thing. This is no way to collaborate with parents!"

I wish I had a video recording of my reaction as Tammy ranted about the guidance department, as it would likely be a great example of "what not to do." I am certain that my mouth hit the floor, and my eyes were bugging out of my head. What the H-E-Double Hockey Sticks is she saying? Shut out? Inaccessible? I could feel the blood rushing to my head as I sat and listened to her rant. What happened next is my example of "what not to do." I took the bait.

"Tammy, I am just completely stunned that you would say this. I have been available to you on a regular basis. I have provided Barry with regular support meetings and been a sounding board for you both. I have to say that I am completely taken aback and stunned that you would say this. I have no idea what you are expecting and why, after all this, you would feel shut out."

Tammy sputtered something else that I do not remember as I was so riled up myself. However, while this was happening, I noticed my co-leader, Gini, sitting near me in the meeting, an enigmatic smile on her face, saying nothing. She had this habit of stroking her long hair while she was thinking, and I saw her slowly doing so. Gini said nothing. Fortunately, the meeting was soon over, and we made our way back to the guidance department.

Once we got back to the guidance department, I catapulted into her office and said, *"What was that?"* Gini knew about all my work with Tammy and Barry. I was so angry and hurt that Tammy had made these comments. I then asked Gini, "Um, why didn't you say anything?" I was imagining that my life was paralleling that of Julius Caesar (*"Et tu, Brute?"*) as Gini had not backed me up.

"Sometimes it is best to say nothing." She smiled and looked at me. What did she mean? "Parents will say things that they don't really mean or later regret. Sometimes, it is best to just let it go or speak to them individually." I think that I left her office still sputtering like a cartoon character and not really understanding until I thought more about it.

In fact, everyone in that meeting *knew* that the guidance department was a very accessible and supportive staff. We had some of the best counselor/student ratios in the state. We were connected to all the academic departments and made efforts to get to know all our students personally. So, what Tammy was saying had no basis. I might have taken a more effective path if I had been wiser or thought more in the moment and WAIT-ed.

This is not the end of the story. The next day, my office phone rang. When I picked it up, I heard Tammy's voice on the other end. To her credit, she took the initiative to follow up on what happened. "I owe you an apology. I don't know what got into me." She described all that I had done for her and for Barry. "I am so very grateful for everything." We were able to talk about how well Barry was doing. All turned out well.

I have never forgotten Tammy, Barry, Gini, and this incident. It informs my thinking today about trying to determine when it is effective to reply to someone and when silence is the better response. We don't always have to answer every accusation or uncivil action from others, and sometimes, not doing so is best. Think W-A-I-T before you just react to someone.

Conclusion

We can be so uncomfortable with silence in social interactions that we feel compelled to say something. This is especially true when it comes to episodes of incivility, and we can feel that silence is "letting them win" or leading others to believe that we agree with them. We tell ourselves, "Don't let them get away with that," and find our lips moving before we have the chance to think.

I am not suggesting to you that it is best to *never* respond. There are other skills that I am reviewing with you that will address ways to speak up for yourself or others. I am simply showing you that, at times, the best response is silence.

There is an old expression that goes something like this. "Don't wrestle with a pig. If you do, you get dirty, and the pig loves it." The same can be true in interactions with others. Some people are out there looking for a fight, and if we speak, we give them the opponent that they are looking for. Don't take the bait.

The Least You Need To Know

- Most of us live in environments that contain some amount of regular noise, and this constant stimulation can be a source of stress.

- Although silence has many benefits, it can also have many drawbacks in interpersonal situations, depending on the context in which it occurs.

- English speakers generally experience significant discomfort with silence and have urges to fill the silence in conversations at four seconds, whereas other cultures can be comfortable with at least double that amount of time.

- Sometimes, silence is the most effective response to an uncivil action or behavior.

- WAIT is an acronym that can help us be mindful of why we are choosing to talk and whether that is effective in that moment.

chapter ten

Active Listening:
Um, Did You Say Something?

I remember being completely tongue-tied and fuzzy-headed. My client was sitting, staring blankly at me as I stumbled over my words. I could hardly emit a complete and coherent sentence. This was not typical behavior for me. At that moment, I wished that I could play charades with my client to communicate my point. I thought, "Better yet, let's just sit in silence. Gosh, that will be so much easier." However, I knew that I had to persevere, and my client patiently waited as I fought my way through the entire fifty-minute session with him. It was painful for us both, I think.

I was a second-year doctoral student in counseling psychology at Michigan State University. During this year of training, we were expected to work twenty hours a week in the counseling center and meet our academic requirements. I also worked twenty hours a week as an academic advisor to help support myself in the program. My life was busy, and I was best friends with caffeine to help me navigate the daily steeplechase that was my schedule.

I had just started my clinical placement, and I was conducting my very first therapy session with an adult client who was a college student. This was not my first experience providing treatment, as I had previous training providing therapy to children and adolescents. College students were simply older adolescents. No big deal, right? Except it felt like one. I was stuck in a feeling of being overwhelmed as I constantly tried to figure out the right thing to say next.

Here is an example of some of the monologue that was jumping around in my head. "Wait, what did he say? Did you hear that correctly? Um, what should you say? What would a therapist say? No, wait, what would an *effective* therapist say in this moment? No, John, stop nodding. You must look like one of those bobblehead statues on the dashboard of the car of your high school friend, Biggy Bickerstaff (I miss those carefree days of driving around the streets of York Beach…). Stop it. Now, focus. Think; *are you thinking?* He's *staring at you! Say something quickly!*"

I won't go on because I'm sure that this is getting too painful for you to even read. Fortunately, the session ended, and I could slink down the hall to leave out the side door. I thought, "Maybe I'll just keep walking and never come back. How far could I get on foot?" But, alas, fleeing was not an option, and I had to go back the next day.

Every one of these sessions was *recorded*, and I had to listen to it again as part of my training. This was horrifying enough, but then I knew that my supervisor, Gersh Kaufman, would also be listening before our supervision meeting. I would have to face the additional humiliations of reliving this session and then having to talk about it. I was sure that this would be another very painful experience.

Fortunately, I was so very wrong. Gersh had trained many a therapist in his day and he was one of those people who made you feel good about yourself as soon as he walked in the room. We talked about what had happened, and I confessed to being caught up in my head about the *right* thing that a *therapist* would say. He reminded me that I was *human* and that my primary task was to *be* a *human*, not the moving target in my mind of whoever that perfect therapist might be.

As I left, he put his hands on my shoulders, looked me straight in the eye, smiled, and said, "Now, *go be human!*" I thought, "I think that I *can* manage that."

Oh, there was one other important detail that I left out. Gersh and I talked about how my client had used the term "collective monologue" in this session. Gersh asked me, "What exactly did he mean by that?" I was so caught up in my own imposter syndrome in that session that I had neglected to ask. Gersh encouraged me to go back and do so. Great! I had my mission, which could be outlined as follows:

- Go be human.
- Ask about "collective monologue."

When I saw my client for the second time, I was a much different person, emphasis on the word "person." I took my mission of being human seriously and pulled it off quite well. I also remembered to ask about my other agenda item, the collective monologue. (Go, me.) My client smiled at the idea that I had remembered something from our first session when I seemed to be completely elsewhere.

My client, "Fred" (not his real name), talked about how difficult it was to connect with other students on campus. "Everyone just wants to talk about themselves." He described groups of students who would focus on a topic in their discussions but not really "discuss" it. Instead, he described how everyone was speaking out loud about her or his own experience.

For example, in discussing midterm exam time, each student would simply say, "Yah, I find that . . . " and the next would say, "My exams were . . . " as another chimed in with "My exam week is most stressful when. . . . " In short, everyone was talking in their own silo, and no one was interacting with each other. Fred called this "the collective monologue."

As a result of my work with Fred, I began to reflect on my own experiences on campus, both as an undergraduate and graduate student. I realized that he was right. Very few students interacted with each other, and very few students applied active listening skills to their discussions.

Who knew that Fred was onto something important in the psychology field? If only he and I had published a paper on this. Rats. We could have made it big. A few years after our work together ended, Charles Derber described these same concepts with the term "conversational narcissism," arguing that greater levels of social disconnection led people to be starved for social support and, therefore, to compete with others for every scrap of attention that they could find.[62] This leads people to shift the focus of conversations constantly back to the fascinating topic that is themselves.

I would argue that the level of narcissism that Derber described has only become more amplified, fueled by social media as well as social and political divisiveness. I hear from friends overseas that these changes are not simply restricted to our continent but are being found increasingly in cultures around the world.

Hence, this is why I am on my mission to make us all more civil, and active listening is one of the key skills to help us do so. So, what is this skill? Keep reading this chapter to find out what it is and how it is a tool you can use to both prevent and deal with incivility.

Listening

When describing the skill of active listening to people, I first describe the basic elements of the skill of *listening*. I make the distinction between *hearing* and *listening*. Hearing is the act of taking in sounds, both verbal and nonverbal, and processing their content by type of sounds and level of importance. *Listen*, according to the Merriam-Webster dictionary, means "to hear something with thoughtful attention; give consideration."[63] This distinction is like the difference between sensation and perception that I teach my students. Sensation is the taking in of sensory information, whereas perception is about making meaning of that information.

Pseudolistening

Sometimes, people will act like they are listening when they are, in fact, not doing so. They may be smiling and looking right at you while you are speaking, perhaps even nodding at appropriate times, which leads you to believe, "Gosh, I must be so fascinating because look at how attentive he (or she) is being." But beware, because what this person might be doing is the sneaky act of "pseudolistening." This leads the speaker to think that they are being listened to when they are, in fact, not.

Pseudolistening is a strategy that people use when they are bored with the speaker or perhaps have heard their story before. It is also a strategy that people in couples, families, and even in the workplace employ quite often. A good friend will sometimes test whether he truly has my attention in a conversation. He will tell his story and then finish what he is saying with the following phrase: "And then I buried the body." If I reply with, "Oh, that is nice," he knows: "Gotcha. You were not listening!"

Aggressive Listening

This is another style of listening that could be perceived as active listening, at least as it starts out. The speaker may say something, and the listener then replies with what appears to be a reply grounded in active listening. However, beware. What is happening is that the listener is setting up the speaker by getting more information so that they can *pounce* on the speaker and criticize their ideas or personality.

As a psychologist who does psychotherapy, I have dealt quite often with aggressive listeners. Certain topics bring out aggressive listening in clients more than others. Whenever I am talking with someone about their use of substances and the impact that this might be having on them, I am bracing myself for this type of response. I remember one client who came to therapy due to anxiety. As we talked about how his alcohol use might be contributing, he said, "So, you think that beer might be contributing to my problems?" I indicated yes. At this point, he became very aggressive and sneered, "Figures. I expected this. You psychologists and your beliefs. Get into the real world. I mean, get a life. I bet that you are going to tell me that *you* never drink and that alcohol is evil!" Fortunately, we were able to go on to have an interesting conversation about how alcohol withdrawal can contribute to anxiety.

Simple Name But Complex Skill

Listening is a seemingly simple gesture that we can offer others to show them that "they matter." Unfortunately, it is increasingly true that people are in what my former client described as the "collective monologue." They are unmotivated to listen to each other and, in fact, will "*cancel*" someone whose opinion or behavior they don't like and who wants to communicate that "you no longer matter." I also hear people railing against "those" people engaged in "cancel culture."

> Listening is a seemingly simple gesture that we can offer others to show them that "they matter."

Here is a late-breaking news flash. We are *all* engaged in some version of cancel culture, and that is one of the major problems in our country at present. People have become increasingly disinterested in listening to others and want to interact in person or via social media to reinforce why their own position is right. This is often a breeding ground for uncivil behavior and leads to greater and greater divisiveness.

I will now get off my soapbox and return to our topic, but I hope to encourage you to use the skills you learn in this book to go out into the world and try to listen more to others, especially those with whom you don't agree. There are different ways to listen, and "active listening" is one of the more important ways to do so. I look forward to sharing these skills with you.

However, don't be lulled into a false sense of security or superiority when you first read its description. One of my first students in Psychology 100 decided that she was going to use the entire semester to battle me like a petulant child. At one point, she said to me, "I can't believe that people get a PhD in this stuff. I mean, it is all just so *obvious*." These skills may seem "simple" or "obvious," but trust me when I say that truly listening and actively listening to someone else takes effort and is not always easy. So, fasten your seatbelts and get ready to *listen* to what I have to say.

Active Listening

The name of this skill suggests that it involves two key components. The first is listening, which we have defined above. The other element is "active," which means that it involves effort. You can't be on the sidelines in this one; rather, you must be "in the game" and show others through your behavior that you are with them.

Early History

Active listening has its early roots in the work of William James, who was known as the father of American psychology. James was part of a movement in early psychology known as functionalism, which sought to understand the mind and the experience of being human in very practical ways. One focus of his writings was the concept of attention, which he described as an active approach to bringing the mind into focus. In his *Principles of Psychology* (1890), he wrote:

> "Attention . . . is the taking possession by the mind, in clear and vivid form, of one out of what seem several simultaneously possible objects or trains of thought. Localization, concentration, of consciousness are of its essence. It implies withdrawal from some things in order to deal effectively with others and is a condition which has a real opposite in the confused, dazed, scatterbrained state which in French is called *distraction*, and *Zerstreutheit* in German."[64]

James also described how difficult it can be to sustain attention in daily life to keep ourselves away from the "confused, dazed, and scatterbrained state" that he noted above. In this same text, he goes on to describe how he could sustain his attention more effectively while reading if he repeated the words to himself internally. Similarly, he found that he was better able to focus on a discussion or presentation if he was actively repeating the things that he was hearing.

> "*I can keep my wandering mind a great deal more closely upon a conversation or a lecture if I actively re-echo to myself the words than if I simply hear them.*"[65]

These ideas would serve as an important foundation for the concept of active listening.

Carl Rogers was an American psychologist who served as president of the American Psychological Association in 1947. He is known as one of the founders of humanistic psychology and developed an approach to clinical work known as client-centered psychotherapy. This approach to treatment was based on the idea that clients have all they need to heal themselves already contained within themselves. The therapist's job is to help the client unlock their full potential and find solutions to their problems by reflecting to the client what they were saying and doing. If the client felt unconditional positive regard, genuineness, and empathy from the therapist, they would be able to unlock the power to heal themselves. Active listening was a key component of this approach to treatment and was a concept first introduced by Carl Rogers and Richard Farson in 1957.[66]

Overview

Active listening became known as a technique that was widely applicable beyond the therapy room and the client-centered approach to treatment. Active listening still is a foundational skill for any therapist in training. However, it is also a skill for anyone in a helping role such as peer mentors or camp counselors. It has also become a foundational skill to improve communication in families as well as supervisors and peers in a work environment.

There are three major components of active listening:

1. First, the listener must pay attention to the speaker (yes, you must pay *attention*).
2. Next, the listener must be able to retain what has been said to them.
3. The final step is responding or reflecting in various ways.

Active listening involves both verbal and nonverbal behavioral strategies that let the speaker know you are interested in what they are saying and want to hear more. I'll tell you more about this in a moment.

The goals of active listening include:

- showing interest in what the speaker is saying and encouraging the speaker to continue

- checking the listener's understanding of what has been said
- reflecting the feelings that the speaker is communicating
- summarizing what the listener has heard to check for accuracy of understanding

Active Listening Skills

The skills of active listening involve what you do both verbally and nonverbally. It is important to communicate your interest in the speaker and invest in the conversation. So, here are the ways to listen actively.[67]

Nonverbally

Be present and nonjudgmental: Woody Allen is known for saying many funny and interesting things. Among my favorites is the following: "80 percent of success is showing up." He was right, but showing up means that we do so *both physically and mentally*. In the modern-day busyness of life, we are accustomed to multitasking. I will sometimes be in a meeting with a new client, and their cell phone will ping. They will *immediately* pick it up and sometimes just begin to text the person back. I stop speaking and wait. Sometimes, they will say, "Go on, I hear you. I must answer Stu." I wait. We then have a conversation about what therapy is for and how their "posse" can roll without them for fifty minutes.

Have you heard of nomophobia? It is also known as **NO MObile phone phobia**.[68] This is an anxiety not simply about losing or damaging your phone but more importantly **FOMO**: fear of missing out in being away from your phone. This is not an official diagnosis but rather a syndrome that has been identified in people existing in an increasingly digitally dependent world.

If we are going to be present, we put our phones and other distractions away. We try to bring our full and complete attention to the current conversation. We also work to let go of any judgment that we might be communicating verbally or nonverbally in order to let the speaker know that they are being respected.

Watch Your Nonverbal Cues

We "speak" with our bodies just as much (or even more) than with our words. How we position our bodies when listening matters a great deal. Some people report that they are most comfortable when they sit with their arms folded in front of them. This may be true, but I point out to people that this is a "closed" body posture that says to the other, "I've already decided no matter what you say." A closed body posture can also communicate judgment. Instead, sit with an open body posture with arms at your side. Smile as you are listening, or at least hold your face in a neutral, accepting position. Leaning your body in communicates interest in what the person is saying. You can also consider nodding at appropriate times (not like the bobblehead I referred to earlier in the chapter). All these things say that you are open and interested in the other.

Keep Appropriate Eye Contact

Although eye contact is a nonverbal behavior, I am separating it out because visual stimuli tend to dominate other senses. This means that eye contact with a speaker when they are talking is critically important and is a major factor in demonstrating interest.

Use the 50/70/4–5 rule. Speakers should make eye contact about 50 percent of the time while they are speaking, and listeners should make eye contact about 70 percent of the time. Hold eye contact for four to five seconds and then slowly look away. Too much or too little eye contact can be disconcerting for the speaker and be perceived as either lack of interest (too little) or threatening (too much).[69]

Verbally

This is really the heart of active listening and involves what you *say* to demonstrate that you are "with" the speaker. Now, what you say will depend upon your goals for the interaction at that moment. You will remember the goals of active listening that I just outlined. Here are some examples of things that a listener might say, depending upon which goal they are targeting.

Demonstrate Interest And Encourage The Speaker To Continue
This form of verbalization encourages the speaker to continue. It might be as simple as making a sound such as "Mm-hmm" or "Oh." Other utterances in this category include "How so?" or "Say more about that." As you can see, these brief verbalizations mean that you simply stay out of the speaker's way and encourage them to continue.

Check For Understanding
Comments in this category indicate you want to be certain that you have the main point of what a person has just said. People can say things like, "So, what I hear you saying is . . ." They might also say, "So, you mean that . . ." or "In other words, you believe that . . ." You may do this quite often when you are listening actively, especially if someone is throwing a great deal of information at you. It is important to mix it up if you are using this strategy. There is nothing more annoying than a listener who keeps saying, "So, what I hear you saying is . . ." "So, what I hear you saying is . . ."

Reflect What The Speaker Is Communicating (In Words Or In Emotions)
With these types of comments, you are echoing what you have heard in either the embedded beliefs or emotions that the speaker has communicated. "It sounds like you have had it with your boss." "Sounds like you think that your coworkers are not supporting you enough, is that right?"

You could also reflect the feeling you hear embedded in the speaker's comments. "You feel unappreciated at work." When I was a high school guidance counselor, I had a colleague who made it quite clear that she did not find the work of the guidance staff to be useful. In one of my first conversations with her, she made a sarcastic joke about guidance counselors. I looked at her completely deadpan and said, "Hmm. You sound angry." We both burst into laughter. From then on, that was our own private joke, and I think that she came to see that counselors are, in fact, useful creatures to have around.

Summarize What The Speaker Has Said

This is a strategy that might be used in parts of a lengthy conversation or at the very end. This goal is designed to help the listener identify what they believe is most important in what has been said and to be sure that this matches with what the speaker intended. "It sounds to me like the things that matter most to you at this point are . . . . " "So, let me tell you what I have heard . . . . " It is always interesting when you get to the end point of a conversation, and you summarize, only to learn that the speaker meant something else. I have, in fact, been in groups (groups of psychologists, no less) who have been talking with each other and *think* that they are on the same page, only to discover after a lengthy period that they have been talking past each other. (Psychologists are people too.)

Barriers To Active Listening

There are many factors that can get in the way of listening and active listening. While the following is not a comprehensive list, it does give you some ideas of what may hamper your ability to listen. I would encourage you to think about which of these might apply to you. I would also urge you to identify what other barriers may exist for you personally. So, without further ado, barriers to listening can include:

- *Distractions.* There can be variables in the physical environment that make it difficult to focus on the speaker and can derail the attention of the listener. For example, our offices used to be in one of the high-rise buildings in Portland. At one point, the owners of the building announced with great excitement that they would be having the stonework on the building resurfaced. Sounds great, right? Okay, now imagine being seven stories up and having scaffolding enveloping your view. Do you know what sounds machines that resurface stone can make? How about the workmen who were wandering around outside our offices, oblivious to our presence and telling "off-color" jokes at a decibel level loud enough to be heard over heavy machinery? Ah, the perfect conditions for a therapist to listen. *Good grief!*

- *Rehearsing.* This barrier to effective listening is rooted in the idea that the listener is more interested in preparing what she or he will say than in what the speaker is saying. The aggressive listener noted above is one example. The "collective monologue" that my client described is another example.

- *Fixing.* In this case, the listener thinks the speaker is asking for help with a problem and replies with advice or suggestions. This is more often the case with men who may see a conversation as having the functional purpose of discussing an issue that needs resolution.[70] This is not true of all men, and more recent literature finds this characteristic as not as universal in men as once believed. However, listeners who reply with "You know what to do" or "I suggest you . . . " when they have not been asked for solutions are engaging in "fixing" behavior.

- *Evaluating.* You might also think of this barrier as judging. As the speaker is speaking, the listener is either saying or doing things that would indicate, "This is not worthwhile" or "How could you be so stupid as to think this?" I have a client who will roll his eyes at me quite frequently, and it has become his trademark. He sometimes utters, "Yes, Dr. O'Brien," at me as he does so. I point out the behavior and note, "Ah, it only took eight minutes this week to get the eye roll." We both laugh. Other clients will be contorting their faces as I am speaking as if to say, "You have no idea what you are talking about." Evaluating can be both verbal and nonverbal.

- *Diverting.* This approach to listening is sometimes used by a listener with the best intentions. Listeners can divert in many ways. They might redirect the conversation to themselves. They could also offer reassurance to the speaker, such as "Oh well, I'm sure that it will all work out." They may minimize the issue with the intent of making the speaker feel better.

  In another example, people often don't know what to say at funerals and memorial services and often say the worst things, such as "At least he is at peace" or "Well, she had a good life." If you remember nothing else from this book, remember this. Be careful what you say at these events, and here are some of my suggestions:

  "I am sorry for your loss."

  "I wish you peace in this difficult time."

  You may want to revisit the WAIT skill described earlier. It is better not to say anything rather than make insensitive comments that the bereaved find aggravating.

- *Interrupting.* "Knock, knock." (Some of you out there are rolling your eyes, I see you. Play along, please. Let's start again.) "Knock, knock." (You: "Who is there?") "Interrupting cow!" (You: "Interrupting co—") "Moooooooooooooo!" I use this all the time with clients who are chronic interrupters, and it illustrates the point. We can interrupt in various ways, including talking over the other person before they can finish or perhaps finishing their sentences when they pause. Research finds that men are more comfortable with interrupting than women, and they are more likely to interrupt women than other men.[71] Those of you who are prone to interrupting (guys, do I have your attention?) should also pay special attention to the chapter on the skill of WAIT.

Applications To Incivility

The skill of active listening has many applications to the topic of incivility. There are two main ideas about how you might use this skill to either prevent an episode of incivility or respond when you are confronted with this behavior from someone else.

Preventing Incivility

There are so many miscommunications and misunderstandings that happen in interactions between people. Many of those miscommunications happen because people are *texting* or *emailing* messages that should never be communicated in electronic formats. I hear about people quitting their jobs or asking for a divorce via text message/email. With very few exceptions, these are not the ways to communicate major decisions.

People are often distracted by many things in their lives and may often be multitasking as they go through their day. If they are not careful, they may fail to realize how their comment may have more than one meaning. I was working with a client recently who said that his girlfriend told him, "If you weren't with me, you'd just be sitting at home." He was highly irritated by this and told her at the time, "No, trust me. I have plenty of things to do with my time!" The topic was dropped at that point.

When we talked about this specific interaction, I highlighted to him that I heard something very different. I told him that I heard her saying, "Isn't your life better with me in it?" While we never found out which one of these she meant, we talked about how she had told him on many occasions how fortunate she felt to have found him.

Active listening is a technique that he could have used in this situation. While his response was not *that* uncivil, it stopped the conversation immediately. Other couples can escalate rather quickly when a miscommunication such as this happens. So, instead of reacting, you can reflect what you hear and highlight the message you are getting. He could have said, "What do you mean?" He could then find out if she meant that (1) you have no life or (2) I hope that you think that your life is better with me in it.

Responding To Incivility
On the other hand, active listening is used differently when you are clear that the other person intends to be uncivil. You can use this skill in a one-on-one conversation to get the person to keep talking in the hopes that they will catch what they are saying. You hope that they will hear what they are saying in the reflection and recognize their incivility. If someone makes a negative comment, you reply with active listening skills.

For example, a friend once said, "Psychologists are just in it for the money." I was stunned but replied, "What do you mean?" He talked about a psychologist who was refusing to release a testing report for a client until the psychologist got paid. "This is just greedy." I continued, "So, she should not be worried about getting paid?" My friend then stopped and changed his tune. "Well, I get it that she needs to get paid, but it is not fair to the client." I highlighted how often we both had times when clients walked away from balances owed and never paid.

You might also use active listening to highlight uncivil comments if they are made in front of a group. Remember, your goal is to be civil but not a doormat. You can change an uncivil person's behavior by using basic behavior change skills. Negative reinforcement is a strategy to increase behavior you want to bring out in your dog (or your coworker—think civil behavior). The other person (or dog) ultimately exhibits the behavior you wish to because they get out of an uncomfortable situation.

When I was a high school guidance counselor, I gave a talk on college exploration to a large group of juniors. We were in the gym, and they were gathered in the bleachers in front of me. This was not the ideal circumstance for classroom management, as many of the students were way above me and looking down on me.

At one point, I was talking about finding the right college, and one student said, "Yeah, well, not Boston College (my alma mater) cuz they suck." He muttered it under his breath and got a few snickers from the kids around him.

I immediately wheeled around and said, "I'm sorry. Did you say something?"

His facial expression quickly changed from a huge grin to a pained look of panic. "Um, no."

I continued walking toward him. "No, I heard you say something. What did you say?"

He got more and more red. "Uh, nothing..."

I kept coming closer and was sure that he was hearing the theme music from Jaws in his head as I slowly but steadily moved toward him. He was now beet red, and I was standing right in front of him. "Happy to have you participate, Mark. Just be sure to speak up if you want to add something." I stared at him with the knowing look of what he had said, and he looked like he wanted to make a run for it. No one gave me any more back talk in that session, and Mark went out of his way to say hello to me for the rest of the year.

Conclusion

When I told my editor that I was going to be writing a chapter on active listening, he replied: "I'm sorry. Did you say something?" Ha, ha! We are all *capable* of listening and active listening at that, but it takes *effort* and *intention* to become active listeners. The skills of active listening require an investment of time, but it is an investment that can pay off in significantly better relationships both at work and at home.

Active listening can be helpful in preventing an episode of incivility that might be based on a misunderstanding of what someone is meaning. This technique can also be a way to highlight for someone what they have just said without answering them back with uncivil words of your own, which then leads to a quickly escalating conflict. I hope that you have *listened* well (unlike my editor) to what I've written here and can find this skill to be of use in responding but not reacting to uncivil comments from others.

The Least You Need To Know

- Listening is a seemingly simple but practically complicated skill in interpersonal communication.

- Greater levels of social disconnection in our society have led to "collective narcissism," wherein people are so starved for attention that they only want to talk about themselves when they have the chance and not really listen (or, as my client called it, the "collective monologue"). Active listening involves several strategies that are used to demonstrate to the speaker that we are not just hearing them but taking in what they are saying.

- There are many factors that can get in the way of really listening to other people.

- Active listening skills can be useful in preventing incivility (due to misunderstanding in discussions) or responding to the uncivil actions of others.

Epilogue

Thankfully, you are now an expert on managing incivility in others and yourself. You feel fully empowered to address any difficulties that come up and have all the skills that you need, right?

Unfortunately, that is not the case. As I've told you, we are all "works in progress" and can face difficulties in our daily lives for which we are not fully prepared. Even the most skilled among us find it challenging at certain times, especially when we are physically or emotionally depleted. There are also specific people or environments that are powerful, and they can overwhelm our ability to cope. That is why we need to constantly be working to practice the skills we have and develop new ones.

I have had the opportunity to work with hundreds of individuals over the course of my nearly thirty-year career in private practice (I started when I was six). Some clients need regular weekly sessions over many years to heal from their trauma history. Other clients may have less severe reasons for seeking treatment, and they engage in therapy for the shorter term. As I wind down treatment with any client, I have learned to ask the question, "And how will you know if you need to return to treatment?" I do this for a good reason.

For many clients, one "dose" of psychotherapy (whether it is six weeks, six months, or six years) may not be enough. I have learned that many clients sometimes feel a sense of shame when calling me to come back. They often tell me that they feel "like I should have learned all I needed to the last time. I failed. I did not implement all we talked about."

At this point, I welcome them to the ranks of the human race. "We are so glad that you are finally joining us!" I remind them that it is very common for people to need a "tune-up" or a reworking of their coping skills due to current life challenges.

And what about you? I remain passionate about helping you, dear reader, with situations of rudeness and incivility that continue to be far too common in our society. I would, in fact, be so pleased if there were no longer a need for a book like mine and people were treating each other in respectful and courteous ways. If that happens, I will gladly find something else to do! That being said, I am not psychic, but I do not see any signs that these behaviors in our society will change any time soon.

Hence, sadly, this book is not the end of the story. I am currently drafting a follow-up book that tackles incivility and rudeness with a specific mindfulness-based approach. For more information, please stay tuned at www.rudenessrehab.com.

For now, I wish you the very best with implementing the *Rudeness Rehab* skills we have reviewed so far. Practice may not make perfect in this case, but hopefully, practice will make things better for you, your loved ones, your community, and our world.

Yours in rudeness recovery,
John

Appendices

Call To Action

I distinctly remember the graduation ceremony. Our internship director at the Dallas VA Medical Center, Dr. Kathy Dohoney, congratulated us on completing the year-long clinical training program that was the capstone to our doctoral degree. "Congratulations," she said. "Now your learning *really* begins!"

I remember thinking, "Wait, whaaaaaaat did she say? Now my learning 'really begins?' What in the heck have I been doing for the last year? No, wait, how about for the last five years in my doctoral program? I have worked so hard and learned so much. That should be enough!"

As I reflect on her statement and my reaction, I realize how accurate she was. Now, over twenty-five years later, I think that her words continue to describe my experience of working with people—there is always more to learn.

In a similar way, you have now made it through this book (congratulations). You have endured all my stories and politely laughed at my jokes (as far as I know). You may be thinking that you are *done* learning about incivility. Alas, as Dr. Dohoney quipped, "Now, your learning *really* begins!"

You have learned the basics about incivility and have the skills to manage rude and angry people lurking in dark corners of your life, waiting to pounce. You have also had the chance to reflect on what you can do differently. However, practicing *civility* in the face of *incivility* remains quite a challenge.

So, why bother? To foment wellness, for one. Remember that we identified the negative impact of stress on your health and wellness. If you do not effectively manage your own incivility or your responses to the uncivil behaviors of others, you can expect negative health consequences that result in increased illness and potentially even a shortened lifespan.

Now, the most important question of all—where do you start? You start at the place where you can have the most impact. Can you guess where that is? Correct. You start with *you*. Remember, you are the lightbulb that must decide if you want to change.

Self-Care And Well-Being

People talk about self-care all the time as something that is important for us to practice. We hear all kinds of recommendations about the best way to take care of ourselves physically and emotionally. Unfortunately, those lofty goals don't always translate into realistic outcomes. So many people are lacking adequate attention to their own well-being, and this has a direct impact on their behavior and stress levels.

I think of self-care as paying attention to our physical and emotional needs in a way that helps us to be our best selves. Self-care is most importantly grounded in wellness behaviors that we do to maintain good health. Some examples of these behaviors include:

- *Nutrition.* The USDA and HHS Dietary Guidelines encourage us to eat a healthy amount of fruits, vegetables, grains, dairy or fortified soy products, and proteins while limiting the amount of alcohol and caffeine we consume.[72] This is all in the context of eating the right number of calories for our age, gender, and activity level.

- *Exercise.* The Centers for Disease Control in the United States urged Americans to "sit less and move more." Guidelines for activity include at least 150 minutes of moderate aerobic activity (brisk walking) or seventy-five minutes of vigorous aerobic activity (running), along with at least two days per week of strength training.[73]
- *Sleep.* The National Sleep Foundation notes that the amount of sleep we require varies based on age.[74] For young adults and adults, seven to nine hours are needed whereas seven to eight hours is suggested for older adults. Your personal sleep requirements may be more or less than the average, but most people will need an amount of sleep in this range to be at their best.

> I think of self-care as paying attention to our physical and emotional needs in a way that helps us to be our best selves.

These three components of physical self-care are essential to maintaining good health. And the more out of balance our bodies are, the more likely we are to engage in uncivil behavior toward others or respond poorly when others act in those ways.

Wellness behaviors (such as those noted above) maintain good health. Well-being incorporates all these behaviors but also includes *how* we emotionally relate to ourselves and others. Some people can be great at wellness behaviors, but they are uncivil to others (and likely themselves). If you want to be more civil, your focus will be on creating well-being for yourself first.

Further Reading

Hopefully, I have helped to pique your interest in being a more civil person, and you want to learn more to support your well-being. If so, here are some suggestions of additional resources to further your own learning about incivility and mindfulness.

Christine Porath:

- *Mastering Community: The Surprising Ways Coming Together Moves Us from Surviving to Thriving* (New York: Balance, 2022).
- *Mastering Civility: A Manifesto for the Workplace* (New York: Balance, 2016).
- *The Cost of Bad Behavior: How Incivility Is Damaging Your Business and What to Do About It*, with Christine Pearson (New York: Portfolio, 2009).

Dan Harris:

- *10% Happier: How I Tamed the Voice in My Head, Reduced Stress Without Losing My Edge, and Found Self-Help That Actually Works–A True Story*, 10th anniversary ed. (New York: Dey Street Books, 2024).
- *Meditation for Fidgety Skeptics: A 10% Happier How-To Book* (New York: Harmony Books, 2017).

Terry Fralich:

- *Cultivating Lasting Happiness: A 7-Step Guide to Mindfulness*, 2nd ed. (Washington, DC: Premier Publishing, 2012).
- *The Five Core Skills of Mindfulness: A Direct Path to More Confidence, Joy and Love* (Eau Claire, WI: PESI, 2013).

John Kabat-Zinn:

- *Full Catastrophe Living: Using the Wisdom of Your Body and Mind to Face Stress, Pain, and Illness,* revised edition (New York: Bantam, 2013).
- *Wherever You Go, There You Are*, 11th edition, (New York, Hachete Go, 2023).
- *Coming to Our Senses: Healing Ourselves and the World Through Mindfulness* (New York: Hachette, 2005).
- *Mindfulness for Beginners: Reclaiming the Present Moment and Your Life* (Louisville, CO: Sounds True, 2011).
- *Mindfulness Meditation for Pain Relief: Practices to Reclaim Your Body and Your Life* (Louisville, CO: Sounds True, 2023).

Psychotherapy And Coaching

Despite the assertions of my student years ago who told me that all of psychology is "obvious" and need not be studied, it is in fact *not* obvious and needs to be studied and practiced if we want to change behavior. Sometimes, we can change our behavior on our own. However, most of us will need some support when we embark on a process of behavior change, especially with more complex behaviors, and we will need to select a coach or therapist to guide us and help us.

People have sometimes asked me about *how* to decide if they need help, and if they do, do they need psychotherapy or coaching? Some clients said in the first session, "Why would I bother paying you? I can get my friends to listen to me for free." My response is that if they can get what they need from their friends for free, go for it. However, if they want confidential support and guidance from a trained professional, they should consider staying in treatment.

Some people think that perhaps they can be their own guide. My suggestion in these cases is that people formulate their own plan for behavior change and give themselves a specified period in which to implement that plan. At the end of the period, they can take an honest look at what has happened. Have they been able to implement significant change on their own? If so, they can continue doing their own work. If not, then they need the support of a professional.

How about the question of coaching versus psychotherapy? I have been trained and worked with clients in both interventions. Some say that psychotherapy is about the past, and coaching is about the present and future. Psychotherapy is about alleviating mental health symptoms, whereas coaching is about personal development and growing positive behaviors. In practice, I think there is way more overlap than difference between these two interventions, but the above distinctions are a good place to start.

How do you find the right person for you? The answer to this question is that the typical psychologist answers, wait for it, "It depends." Remember that psychotherapy may or may not be covered by insurance, whereas coaching is not. If you are seeking psychotherapy and want to use your insurance, you must be sure to select someone who takes your plan. Other factors to consider include:

- *Location.* Do you want to see someone in person, or is virtual okay? If you are open to virtual meetings, you will have a larger population of providers to choose from.

- *Expertise.* Find someone who has training and expertise in what you wish to target.

- *Gender.* Do you prefer to see someone of a particular gender? Does that matter to you?

- *Personal qualities.* You want to find someone with whom you can relate and whom you believe can truly understand you in your situation. Do you want someone who shares your racial or cultural background, religious background, sexual orientation, or gender identity? Consider the personal qualities (if any) that you want in your provider.

- *Voice.* I have always suggested that people call the person's voicemail or find a recording of that person. You will have a gut reaction when you hear someone's voice that will tell you "yes" or "no." I encourage you to listen to that reaction.

This discussion is not comprehensive and is meant only as a general guide. However, my point is that the process of choosing a therapist or coach is not like deciding if you want your groceries in "paper or plastic." You need to put effort and energy into the process of selecting the person who will be right for you. Take your time and choose wisely. I believe that the relationship you develop with that person will be *the most important part* of your healing and development journey.

And Now Your Learning Truly Begins

As I told you upfront, I can be an uncivil person. Every day, as I get out of bed and my feet hit the floor, I consider who I want to be. Most days (though not all), I do a pretty good job (but not perfect). You now know that you have the same choice. Who will you be? The rest is up to you.

As I send you off into the world, I think of the Dalai Lama, who said, "Anger and hatred are signs of weakness, while compassion is a sure sign of strength."

Choosing to be civil, especially in the face of uncivil behavior from others, is no easy task. However, it is a choice worth making for your own health and to be the best self you can be for those around you.

Acknowledgments

"Don't let the sun go down without saying thank you to someone and without admitting to yourself that absolutely no one gets this far alone."
—Stephen King

would like to take this opportunity to thank all the people in my life, past and present, who have helped in my development as a clinician, teacher, and writer but most importantly, as a person. Thank you to:

- My family and friends, who helped me believe in myself and that I have something of value to offer to my readers and who encouraged me to write this book.
- My mentors, teachers, and supervisors, who guided me in growing my self-awareness throughout the years so that I can be of better help to others.
- My editors and publisher, who supported me in this journey, especially when I lost faith in myself and thought I could not finish.

About The Author

John M. O'Brien is a professional speaker, consultant, and executive coach based in Portland, Maine. With over three decades of experience, John is a seasoned expert in guiding individuals through significant life transitions. Through his programs, John equips audiences with tangible skills and concrete tools that empower them to swiftly reduce stress levels and enhance personal wellness, leading to immediate positive transformation.

He is a licensed psychologist in private practice since 1998, providing individual psychotherapy and consultation. In addition, John has served as an adjunct faculty member at the University of Maine at Augusta since 2000, where he teaches courses in psychology, trauma, and addiction-related topics.

John provides coaching and consulting to individuals and groups, including executive assessment, leadership development, and health and wellness promotion across a variety of professions, including business, health care, law, and financial services. He is an International Coaching Federation Associate Certified Coach (ICF ACC) and National Board Certified Health & Wellness Coach through the National Board for Health & Wellness Coaching. He is a former president of the Maine Psychological Association and has served in numerous positions in leadership within the American Psychological Association, most recently in the Society of Consulting Psychology.

John works with organizations that want to create low-stress work environments to ignite employee engagement, increase productivity, and strengthen profitability. You can find out more about him at www.activatesuccess.org.

In his spare time, John enjoys motorcycling, skiing, biking (especially his Peloton), and further developing his German skills. He also serves as full-time staff to his gifted cat, Shahdi.

Works Cited And Author's Notes

[1] *Stress in America 2023: A Nation Recovering from Collective Trauma*, American Psychological Association, November 2023, https://www.apa.org/news/press/releases/stress/2023/collective-trauma-recovery.

[2] "Are You Suffering from Post-COVID Rudeness Syndrome?" College of Law, April 24, 2023, https://www.collaw.edu.au/news/2023/04/04/are-you-suffering-from-post-covid-rudeness-syndrome.

[3] Howard J. Shaffer and Stephanie B. Jones, *Quitting Cocaine: The Struggle against Impulse*, (Lexington, MA: Lexington Books, 1989).

[4] C.L. Porath and C.M. Pearson, "The Cost of Bad Behavior." *Organizational Dynamics*, 2010, 39(1), 64–71. https://psycnet.apa.org/doi/10.1016/j.orgdyn.2009.10.006

[5] Dan Harris, *10% Happier: How I Tamed the Voice in My Head, Reduced Stress Without Losing My Edge, and Found Self-Help That Actually Works–A True Story*, 10th-anniversary ed. (New York: Dey Street Books, 2024).

[6] Nicole Celestine, "The Science of Happiness in Positive Psychology 101," PositivePsychology.com, modified March 11, 2024, https://positivepsychology.com/happiness/.

[7] "Life Expectancy in the U.S. Dropped for the Second Year in a Row in 2021," National Center for Health Statistics, Centers for Disease Control and Prevention, August 31, 2022, https://www.cdc.gov/nchs/pressroom/nchs_press_releases/2022/20220831.htm.

[8] Martha Henriques, "Can the Legacy of Trauma Be Passed Down the Generations?" BBC.com, March 26, 2019, https://www.bbc.com/future/article/20190326-what-is-epigenetics.

[9] Rachel Yehuda, et al., "Holocaust Exposure Induced Intergenerational Effects on FKBP5 Methylation," *Biological Psychiatry* 80, no. 5 (September 1, 2016): 372–380, https://doi.org/10.1016/j.biopsych.2015.08.005.

[10] R.C. Kessler, P. Berglund, O. Demler, R. Jin, K.R. Merikangas, E.E. Walters, "Lifetime prevalence and age-of-onset distributions of DSM-IV disorders in the National Comorbidity Survey Replication," *Arch Gen Psychiatry*. 2005 Jun;62(6):593-602

[11] Maria Ciccarelli, Mark. D. Griffiths, Giovana Nigro, Marina Cosenza, "Decision making, cognitive distortions and emotional distress: A comparison between pathological gamblers and healthy controls," *Journal of Behavior Therapy and Experimental Psychiatry*, August 16, 2016, 54, 204-210.

[12] "Table 2.25B – Alcohol Use in Lifetime: Among People Aged 12 or Older; by Age Group and Demographic Characteristics, Percentages, 2021 and 2022," 2022 NSDUH Detailed Tables, Substance Abuse and Mental Health Services Administration, November 13, 2023, https://www.samhsa.gov/data/sites/default/files/reports/rpt42728/NSDUHDetailedTabs2022/NSDUHDetailedTabs2022/NSDUHDetTabsSect2pe2022.htm#tab2.25b.

[13] Kevin P. Hill, *Marijuana: The Unbiased Truth About the World's Most Popular Weed*, (Center City, MN: Hazelden Publications, 2015).

[14] H. R. Treloar, "Relations Among Caffeine Consumption, Smoking, Smoking Urge, and Subjective Smoking Reinforcement in Daily Life," *Journal of Caffeine Research*. 2014, 4 (3) 93-99. https://www.ncbi.nlm.nih.gov/pmc/articles/PMC4158991/#:~:text=One%20plausible%20explanation%20is%20that%20caffeine%20and%20tobacco,propensity%20to%20boost%20energy%2C%20concentration%2C%20alertness%2C%20and%20mood

[15] Stephen Babb, Ann Malarcher, Gillian Schauer, Kat Asman, and Ahmed Jamal, "Quitting Smoking Among Adults — United States, 2000–2015," *Morbidity and Mortality Weekly Report* 65, no. 52 (January 6, 2017): 1457–1464, http://dx.doi.org/10.15585/mmwr.mm6552a1.

[16] B. Z. Mahon and D. Kemmerer, "Interactions between language, thought, and perception: Cognitive and neural perspectives," *Cognitive Neuropsychology*, 2020, 37 (5-6), 235-240.

[17] Kendra Cherry, "What Is the Negativity Bias?" Verywell Mind, updated November 13, 2023, https://www.verywellmind.com/negative-bias-4589618.

[18] Dorothy Firman, "Peace: A Job for One," *Living a Life of Purpose* (blog), *Psychology Today*, December 19, 2014, https://www.psychologytoday.com/us/blog/living-a-life-of-purpose/201412/peace-a-job-for-one.

[19] J.C. Barefoot and R.B. Williams, *Hostility and Health,* In: *Handbook of Cardiovascular Behavioral Medicine*, (Springer, New York, NY: 2022). https://doi.org/10.1007/978-0-387-85960-6_20

[20] Merriam-Webster.com Dictionary, s.v. "hostility," accessed April 11, 2024, https://www.merriam-webster.com/dictionary/hostility.

[21] John C. Barefoot and Redford B. Williams, "Hostility and Health" in *Handbook of Cardiovascular Behavioral Medicine,* eds. Shari R. Waldstein, Willem J. Kop, Edward C. Suarez, William R. Lovallo, and Leslie I. Katzel, (New York: Springer, 2022), 503–524, https://doi.org/10.1007/978-0-387-85960-6_20.

[22] Merriam-Webster.com Dictionary, s.v. "awareness," accessed April 11, 2024, https://www.merriam-webster.com/dictionary/awareness.

[23] Enrique Rubio, "Increasing Your Self-Awareness: The Johari Window," October 20, 2015, LinkedIn, https://www.linkedin.com/pulse/increasing-your-self-awareness-johari-window-enrique/.

[24] Merriam-Webster.com Dictionary, s.v. "reaction," accessed April 11, 2024, https://www.merriam-webster.com/dictionary/reaction.

[25] Merriam-Webster.com Dictionary, s.v. "respond," accessed April 11, 2024, https://www.merriam-webster.com/dictionary/respond.

[26] David G. Myers and C. Nathan DeWall, *Psychology in Modules*, 13th ed. (New York: Worth Publishers, 2021).

[27] Ronald D. Siegel, *The Mindfulness Solution: Everyday Practices for Everyday Problems* (New York: Guilford Press, 2009), p. 32–33.

[28] Mark Williams and Danny Penman, *Mindfulness: An Eight-Week Plan to Finding Peace in a Frantic World*, (New York: Rodale Books, 2011), p.165–166.

[29] Christopher K. Germer, Ronald D. Siegel, and Paul R. Fulton, eds., *Mindfulness and Psychotherapy*, 1st ed. (New York: Guilford Press, 2005), p. 7.

[30] Dan Harris, *10% Happier: How I Tamed the Voice in My Head, Reduced Stress Without Losing My Edge, and Found Self-Help That Actually Works–A True Story*, (New York: Dey Street Books, 2014).

[31] M. Linehan, *Dialectical Behavior Therapy of Borderline Personality Disorder*, (New York: The Guilford Press, 1993)

[32] Arlin Cuncic, "How to Embrace Radical Acceptance," Verywell Mind, updated November 3, 2022, https://www.verywellmind.com/what-is-radical-acceptance-5120614.

[33] Steven Hayes, K..Strosahl, and K. Wilson, *Acceptance and Commitment Therapy: The Process and Practice of Mindful Change 2nd Edition*, (New York: The Guilford Press, 2011)

[34] Russ Harris, *ACT Made Simple: An Easy-To-Read Primer on Acceptance and Commitment Therapy*, 2nd ed. (Oakland, CA: New Harbinger Publications, Inc: 2019).

[35] Steven C. Hayes, Kirk D. Strosahl, and Kelly G. Wilson, *Acceptance and Commitment Therapy: An Experiential Approach to Behavior Change*, (New York: Guilford Press, 1999).

[36] Jalāl ad-Dīn Muhammad Rūmī, "The Guest House", translated by Coleman Barks, *The Essential Rumi*, (Las Vegas, NV: Castle Books, 1997)

[37] Linehan, Dialectical Behavior Therapy of Borderline Personality Disorder, 1993.

[38] Terry Fralich, *Cultivating Lasting Happiness: A 7-Step Guide to Mindfulness*, 2nd ed. (Washington, DC: Premier Publishing, 2012). p. 90.

[39] Harris, *10% Happier* and Dan Harris, et al., *Meditation for Fidgety Skeptics: A 10% Happier How-To Book*, (New York: Harmony Books, 2017).

[40] Jon Kabat-Zinn, *Full Catastrophe Living: Using the Wisdom of Your Body and Mind to Face Stress, Pain, and Illness*, rev. ed. (New York: Bantam,

2013), and Jon Kabat-Zinn, *Wherever You Go, There You Are*, 11th ed. (New York, Hachete Go, 2023).

[41] Terry Fralich, *Cultivating Lasting Happiness: A 7-Step Guide to Mindfulness*, 2nd ed. (Washington, DC: Premier Publishing, 2012).

[42] R. Eichinger, "Neuroscience for Coaching Leaders," Paper presented at the annual meeting of the Society of Industrial and Organizational Psychology. October 19, 2017.

[43] W. Morgan and S. Morgan "Cultivating attention and empathy," Germer, C., Siegel, R. & Fulton, P. (Eds) Mindfulness and Psychotherapy, (New York: Guilford Press, 2005) p. 81.

[44] Diana Hill, "What Are the Benefits of Compassion?" *From Striving to Thriving* (blog), *Psychology Today*, April 10, 2023, https://www.psychologytoday.com/us/blog/from-striving-to-thriving/202304/what-are-the-benefits-of-compassion.

[45] Elaine Mead, "What Is Mindful Self-Compassion?" PositivePsychology.com, modified March 15, 2024, https://positivepsychology.com/mindful-self-compassion/#a-look-at-the-research.

[46] Neel Burton, "Does True Altruism Exist?" *Hide and Seek* (blog), *Psychology Today*, revised August 9, 2020, https://www.psychologytoday.com/us/blog/hide-and-seek/201203/does-true-altruism-exist.

[47] Kori D. Miller, "What Is Kindness in Psychology?" PositivePsychology.com, modified March 15, 2024, https://positivepsychology.com/character-strength-kindness/.

[48] David R. Hamilton, *The Five Side Effects of Kindness: This Book Will Make You Feel Better, Be Happier & Live Longer*, (London: Hay House UK, 2021).

[49] Terry Fralich, *The Five Core Skills of Mindfulness: A Direct Path to More Confidence, Joy and Love*, (Eau Claire, WI: PESI, 2013).

[50] Martin Zucker, "Grounding the Human Body: The Healing Benefits of Earthing," chopra.com, September 7, 2019, https://chopra.com/articles/grounding-the-human-body-the-healing-benefits-of-earthing.

[51] Zamfira Parincu and Tchiki Davis, "What Are Grounding Techniques?" *Click Here for Happiness* (blog), *Psychology Today*, August 31, 2022, https://www.psychologytoday.com/us/blog/click-here-for-happiness/202208/what-are-grounding-techniques.

52 Matthew Tull, "Grounding Techniques for Post-Traumatic Stress Disorder," Verywell Mind, updated April 16, 2021, https://www.verywellmind.com/grounding-techniques-for-ptsd-2797300.

53 Lisa M. Najavits, *Seeking Safety: A Treatment Manual for PTSD and Substance Abuse*, (New York: The Guilford Press, 2002).

54 Najavits, *Seeking Safety. A Treatment Manual for PTSD and Substance Abuse*, (New York: The Guilford Press, 2002).

55 Richard Rogers and Oscar Hammerstein II, "My Favorite Things," Williamson Music, 1959.

56 Kendra Cherry, "How Sensory Adaptation Works," Verywell Mind, updated February 25, 2024, https://www.verywellmind.com/what-is-sensory-adaptation-2795869.

57 Samoon Ahmad, "How Constant Noise Keeps Us Chronically Stressed," *Balanced* (blog), *Psychology Today*, December 1, 2022, https://www.psychologytoday.com/us/blog/balanced/202212/how-constant-noise-keeps-us-chronically-stressed.

58 Sarah Garone, "8 Physical and Mental Health Benefits of Silence, Plus How to Get More of It," Healthline, updated September 24, 2021, https://www.healthline.com/health/mind-body/physical-and-mental-health-benefits-of-silence.

59 Janelle Cox, "The Hidden Benefits of Silence," PsychCentral, updated April 29, 2022, https://psychcentral.com/blog/the-hidden-benefits-of-silence.

60 Carrie Shearer, "The Cultural Implications of Silence Around the World," RW3 CulturalWizard, August 20, 2020, https://www.rw-3.com/blog/cultural-implications-of-silence.

61 Lennox Morrison, "The Subtle Power of Uncomfortable Silences," BBC.com, July 18, 2017, https://www.bbc.com/worklife/article/20170718-the-subtle-power-of-uncomfortable-silences.

62 Charles Derber, *The Pursuit of Attention: Power and Ego in Everyday Life*, (Oxford: Oxford University Press, 2000).

63 Merriam-Webster.com Dictionary, s.v. "listen," accessed April 11, 2024, https://www.merriam-webster.com/dictionary/listen.

64 William James, *Principles of Psychology*, (New York: Holt, 1890), 403–404.

[65] James, *Principles of Psychology*, 447.

[66] Carl Ransom Rogers and Richard Evans Farson, *Active Listening*, (Chicago: University of Chicago, 1957).

[67] Arlin Cuncic, "7 Active Listening Techniques for Better Communication," Verywell Mind, updated February 12, 2024, https://www.verywellmind.com/what-is-active-listening-3024343.

[68] Kendra Cherry, "Nomophobia: The Fear of Being Without Your Phone," Verywell Mind, updated August 16, 2023, https://www.verywellmind.com/nomophobia-the-fear-of-being-without-your-phone-4781725.

[69] Arlin Cuncic, "How to Overcome Eye Contact Anxiety," Verywell Mind, updated December 6, 2023, https://www.verywellmind.com/how-do-i-maintain-good-eye-contact-3024392.

[70] Rob Kendall, "5 Ways Men and Women Talk Differently," *Blamestorming* (blog), *Psychology Today*, December 15, 2016, https://www.psychologytoday.com/us/blog/blamestorming/201612/5-ways-men-and-women-talk-differently.

[71] Adrienne B. Hancock and Benjamin A. Rubin, "Influence of Communication Partner's Gender on Language," *Journal of Language and Social Psychology* 34, no. 1 (January 2015): 46–64, https://psycnet.apa.org/doi/10.1177/0261927X14533197.

[72] *Dietary Guidelines for Americans, 2020–2025, Executive Summary*, U.S. Department of Agriculture and U.S. Department of Health and Human Services, December 2020, https://www.dietaryguidelines.gov/sites/default/files/2021-03/DGA_2020-2025_ExecutiveSummary_English.pdf.

[73] "How Much Physical Activity Do Adults Need?" Centers for Disease Control and Prevention, last reviewed June 22, 2022, https://www.cdc.gov/physicalactivity/basics/adults/index.htm.

[74] Max Hirshkowitz et al., "National Sleep Foundation's Updated Sleep Duration Recommendations: Final Report," *Sleep Health: Journal of the National Sleep Foundation* 1, no. 4 (December 2015): 233–243, https://doi.org/10.1016/j.sleh.2015.10.004.